Values for a New Generation

Great Thinkers Discuss What Truly Matters in Life

The Borromean Lecture Series

ISBN: 0988650932
ISBN-13: 978-0988650930

Significance Press
200 Park Avenue, 26th Floor
New York, NY 10166
www.SignificancePress.com

To Mom, Dad, Jack, Rody, Martha, Cort, Mary, Bob, Jan, Geoffrey and Peter—
People who believe in the ideals reflected in these pages.

CONTENTS

Acknowledgements

I wish to thank the individuals who were instrumental in producing this work. Without their efforts, the words about life and values herein could never have reached a broader audience.

I extend my gratitude to Dominic Cavello, among St. Charles' most dedicated and impactful educators, and to Lou Fabro, who were instrumental in the production of the Borromean Lecture Series, and to James Lower, for his ongoing support.

I wish also to acknowledge the work of those at The Dilenschneider Group and Significance Press – especially Joe Tessitore, Joan Avagliano, Joe Pisani, and Patrick Malone - who compiled these speeches and assembled them here.

I finally offer my most profound appreciation to Michael Novak; the Late Cardinal Avery Dulles, S.J.; Joel Klein; F. Russell Hittinger; Archbishop Celestino Migliore; Father John I. Jenkins, C.S.C; Carl Anderson, Father Robert F. O'Toole, S.J.; Father Jeffrey von Arx, S.J.; and Bill McGurn, who traveled to Columbus and participated in the Borromean Lecture Series as speakers. The words and examples of these esteemed individuals, each one remarkable in his own right, provide sorely needed direction in America in the 21st century.

FOREWORD

What can you say about a society where 75 percent of young people believe morality and virtue are declining?

Do young people know something we don't? Are their moral compasses more attuned to right and wrong than the moral compasses of our leaders in government, politics, the media and business?

Three out of four members of the Millennial Generation -- those 78 million Americans who are 18 to 37 -- have a pessimistic view about virtue in the United States.

The poll numbers, sad to say, seem to get worse every year, despite hand-wringing by our religious and political leaders, our educators and commentators. The situation can, quite simply, seem hopeless. If this is the world that the Baby Boomers bequeathed to the next generation, we have big problems because it seems as if the Millennial Generation has inherited a moral wasteland

Nevertheless, I'm convinced there is a reason to be optimistic, and that reason is the Millennial Generation, which despite its challenges seems to display an inextinguishable hope.

They believe the world can be a better place tomorrow than it is today even though they have difficulty finding jobs and paying off student loans. And while it has been widely reported that their lives won't be as prosperous as their parents, they are neverthe-less optimistic.

Yes, these young people, who cross different so-cio-economic groups, possess one telling virtue that has characterized America since its founding – hope. They possess the American spirit -- a quality that can be found no where else in the world. And it's our job as parents, educators, mentors and friends to inspire them as America moves into the 21st century.

That is what this book is about – inspiring and moving the next generation to a still higher level.

"Values for a New Generation – Great Thinkers Discuss What Truly Matters in Life" is a compilation of some of the finest speeches ever given by some of the nation's greatest thinkers on such topics as virtue, morality, doing the right thing, standing alone in the face of opposition, resisting the crowd and cultivating those most profound of all virtues – integrity, honesty and loyalty

These lectures were given to high school stu-dents by such distinguished leaders and thinkers as the late Cardinal Avery Dulles, S.J.; philosopher, jour-nalist and diplomat Michael Novak; Joel I. Klein, former chancellor of New York City public schools; the Rev. John I. Jenkins, C.S.C., president of Univer-sity of Notre Dame; and columnist and news execu-tive William McGurn, among others.

All of them participated in the "Borromean Lec-ture Series" over more than a decade, and all of them shared their wisdom with some 700 high school students at St. Charles Borromeo Preparatory School in Columbus, Ohio. In less than an hour, they each tried to instill in these students an enduring sense of what is truly important in life, beyond materialism, prestige, possessions, pleasure, and the many ephemeral enticements that our society dangles before us as having lasting value.

It's my belief that those thousands of young men who listened to these talks were changed for the better and that they, in turn, as adults changed the lives of others they encountered. At least that was my hope when I began the series more than a decade ago with then-headmaster Dominic Cavello.

You see, St. Charles was my high school, and I can still remember the teachers who had a lasting impact on my adolescent mind, the teachers who said something that resonated with me, the teachers who shared an eternal truth that I carried with me into adulthood which changed me forever. This sense of mission that I acquired from my years at St. Charles inspired me to initiate the series in the persistent hope, against the odds, perhaps, that we can turn our nation's moral compass around.

I encourage you to read this collection of speeches about good and evil, about the importance of freedom and responsibility, about community and family.

A decade ago, Cardinal Dulles told the young men of St. Charles: "Civilization, once achieved, does not automatically perpetuate itself. We are always at the brink of a precipice, in imminent danger of relapsing into barbarism."

I firmly believe it is our responsibility to stop this trend toward barbarity.

- Robert L. Dilenschneider, October 2013
Founder and Principal, The Dilenschneider Group
Class of 1961, St. Charles Preparatory School

1

Michael Novak

on
Faith and the American Founding

*"Reason and faith are the two wings by which the
American eagle took flight."*

It is really an honor and a privilege to speak at this
school. You represent something very special in the
world. It is a rare school today that insists on such
high standards as St. Charles does. St. Charles insists on a
rigorous, mandatory course of Latin, which means a percentage of young men will try and fail. Still, St. Charles
insists that it is not going to lower its standards. It keeps
its standards up there and forces young men to reach.

That is terrific. It is a rare thing. I really commend
you. And it was no wonder to me, then, that one of your
graduates, Mr. Dilenschneider, whom I have been
privileged to call a friend, forty years after he graduated, thought so well of the experience here that he
wanted to do something for the school.

I have met so many others who have spoken of
the same experience. Something terrific has happened

here that has made people want to stay in contact and contribute. I really commend you. It could not be at a more important time in our nation's history.

I also want to take the occasion to greet a dear friend of mine, from Ohio Dominican across the way, Sister Camilla, and John Kasich, former congressman from this area, another good man, and a real spokesman for what is right and true in the American experiment. But mostly I wanted to greet again the young men who were here earlier today. So much is going to rest with them in the next few years.

* * *

My subject is what I call the "second wing of the eagle." That refers to the Jewish and Christian influences on America. I want to tell six stories which bring to light the role that faith—the humble faith of our founders—played in the founding of the United States. Most of the stories about our founding concentrate on the role of reason—the Enlightenment and John Locke—but that's because most of our historians are not very religious. Some of my stories you may never have heard, but they are there, and there are lots more.

Before I get into that, though, I thought I would talk a little bit about the events of September 11th. In a way, nothing in a long time, surely not the last ten to fifteen years, has brought us as close to the understanding of reality present at the time of the founding as the events of September 11th.

On that day my wife and I were in Europe, in Bratislava, and in Prague the next day, as the events unfolded. People there were just as stricken with grief as we were; many had tears running down their faces for days, and got no work done as they watched television, trying to understand. They wanted the Americans they met to know how deeply they felt. The common people of Europe overwhelmingly felt instant sympathy for the people of the United States.

I won't say this was quite the reaction among journalists and the political class. Some of them were writing, "We deserved it" and "It was about time"; but that is not the way the vast 80 percent majority felt.

As a German ship passed an American naval vessel off the European coast, to the Americans' astonishment, they saw the U.S. flag flying on the German vessel. All the men in full dress uniform were standing at attention on deck, and over the side of the ship they unfurled a huge white sheet. On it in block lettering it said, "We stand with you." They saluted, and the Americans passed. Really it touched the hearts of the young men on that American ship. They did not expect that. But that was generally the feeling in Europe.

Football games—that means soccer—were canceled in Slovakia. In Prague there was a three-minute moment of silence. Whistles blew at 11-something in the morning, and people stopped right in their tracks in Wenceslas Square. It was like they suddenly went into that pantomime of nobody moving. Trucks stopped for three minutes. There was a huge service in St. Vidas' Cathedral, an ecumenical service.

You would have thought it was America. Of course all of those countries have extended family over here. We have to remember that the American family comes from everywhere. We are a planetary people, so to speak.

* * *

How long are we going to keep this experiment, this America? We are "testing whether this nation can long endure," Lincoln said at Gettysburg. We're still testing. Is America a meteor that blazed across the heavens and is now exhausted? Or rather is our present moral fog a transient time of trial, those hours cold and dark before the ramparts' new gleaming? Are we near our end or at a beginning?

In answer to these questions, I want to tell six brief stories to illustrate the religious principles of the American founding. For a hundred years scholars have stressed the principles that come from the Enlightenment and from John Locke in particular. But there are also first principles that come to us from Judaism and Christianity, especially from Judaism. Indeed, it is important to recognize that most of what our founders talked about (when they talked politically) came from the Jewish Testament, not the Christian. The Protestant Christians who led the way in establishing the principles of this country were uncommonly attached to the Jewish Testament.

Scholars often mistakenly refer to the god of the founders as a deist god. But the founders talked about God in terms that are radically Jewish: Creator, Lawgiver, Governor, Judge, and Providence. These were the names they most commonly used for Him, notably in the Declaration of Independence. For the most part, these are not names that could have come from the Greeks or Romans, but only from the Jewish Testament. Perhaps the founders avoided Christian language because they didn't want to divide one another, since different colonies were founded under different Christian inspirations. In any case, all found common language in the language of the Jewish Testament. It is important for citizens today whose main inspiration is the Enlightenment and Reason to grasp the religious elements in the founding, which have been understated for a hundred years.

For these principles are important to many fellow citizens, and they are probably indispensable to the moral health of the Republic, as Washington taught us in his Farewell Address: "Of all the dispositions and habits which lead to political prosperity, religion and morality are indispensable supports."

Reason and faith are the two wings by which the American eagle took flight.

If I stress the second wing, the Jewish especially, it is because scholars have paid too much attention to Jefferson in these matters and ignored the other one hundred top founders. For instance, we've ignored John Witherspoon, the president of Princeton, "the most influential professor in the history of America," who taught one President (Madison stayed an extra year at Princeton to study with him), a vice president, three Supreme Court justices including the chief justice, twelve members of the Continental Congress, five delegates to the Constitutional Convention, fourteen members of the State Conventions (that ratified the Constitution). During the revolution, many of his pupils were in positions of command in the American forces. We've ignored Dr. Benjamin Rush of Pennsylvania, John Wilson of Pennsylvania, and a host of others.

I want to quote from some of the founders to give you a taste of the religious energy behind the founding.

Jefferson's Sanction

Here is my first little story, an anecdote recorded by a minister of the time:

> "President Jefferson was on his way to church on a Sunday morning with his large red prayer book under his arm when a friend querying him after their mutual good morning said which way are you walking Mr. Jefferson. To which he replied to Church Sir. You going to church Mr. J. You do not believe a word in it. Sir said Mr. J. No nation has ever yet existed

or been governed without religion. Nor can be. The Christian religion is the best religion that has ever been given to man and I as chief Magistrate of this nation am bound to give it the sanction of my example. Good morning Sir."

Note what Jefferson is saying. He didn't say he believed in the Christian God; he evaded that point. But Jefferson did agree with what all his colleagues in the founding thought, that a people cannot maintain liberty without religion. Here is John Adams in 1776:

"I sometimes tremble to think that although we are engaged in the best cause that ever employed the human heart, yet the prospect of success is doubtful, not for want of power or of wisdom but of virtue."

The founding generation had no munitions factory this side of the ocean, and yet they were facing the most powerful army and the largest navy in the world. Besides, their unity was fragile. The people of Virginia did not like the people of Massachusetts. The people of Massachusetts did not think highly of the people of Georgia. Reflecting on this point, President Witherspoon, who had just arrived from Scotland in 1768 and was not at first in favor of it, gave a famous sermon in April 1776 supporting independence two months before July 4. His text was read in all 500 Presbyterian churches in the colonies and widely reproduced. Witherspoon argued that although hostilities had been going on for two years, the king still did not understand that he could easily have divided the colonies and ended the hostilities. That the king didn't do so showed that he was not close enough to know how to govern the Americans.

If they were to stick together with people they didn't particularly like, the Americans needed virtues of tolerance, civic spirit, and a love of the common good. Further, because the new nation couldn't compete in armed power, the colonists depended on high moral qualities in their leaders and on devotion in the people. In order to win, for instance, Washington had to avoid frontal combat, and to rely on the moral endurance of his countrymen year after year. To this end, Washington issued an order that any soldier who used profane language would be drummed out of the army. He impressed upon his men that they were fighting for a cause that demanded a special moral appeal, and he wanted no citizen to be shocked by the language and behavior of his troops. The men must show day-by-day that they fought under a special moral covenant.

Now think of our predicament today. How many people in America today understand the four key words that once formed a great mosaic over the American Republic? *Truth*, we "hold these truths"; *Liberty,* "conceived in liberty"; *Law,* "liberty under law"; and *Judge,* "appealing to the Supreme Judge of the world for the rectitude of our intentions." On the face of things, our founders were committing treason. In the eyes of the world, they were seditious. They appealed to an objective world, and beyond the eyes of an objective world, they appealed to the Supreme Judge for the rectitude of their intentions. That great mosaic, which used to form the beautiful, colorful apse over the American Republic, in this nonjudgmental age has fallen to the dust. It is disassembled in a thousand pieces. Fewer every year remember how it used to look.

Congress in Prayer

In the first days of September 1774, from every region, members of the First Continental Congress were riding dustily toward Philadelphia, where they hoped to remind King George III of the rights due to them as Englishmen. That's all they were claiming: the rights of Englishmen. And they wanted to remind King George that they were wards of the king. They weren't founded by the Parliament, they were founded by the king, and they resented the Parliament taxing them. The Parliament had nothing to do with their relationship to the king, they thought. Yet, as these delegates were gathering, news arrived that the king's troops were shelling Charlestown and Boston, and rumors flew that the city was being sacked, and robbery and murder were being committed. Those rumors turned out not to be true, but that's the news they heard. Thus, as they gathered, the delegates were confronted with impending war. Their first act as a Continental Congress was to request a session of prayer.

Mr. Jay of New York and Mr. Rutledge of South Carolina immediately spoke against this motion. They said that Americans are so divided in religious sentiments, some Episcopalians, some Quakers, some Anabaptists, some Presbyterians, and some Congregationalists, all could not join in the same act of prayer. Sam Adams rose to say he's no bigot, and could hear a prayer from any gentleman of piety and virtue as long as he is a patriot. "I've heard of a certain Reverend Duché," he said, speaking of the rector of Christ Church down the street from where they were meeting. "People say he's earned that character." Adams moved that the same be asked to read prayers before Congress on the next morning. And the motion carried.

Thus it happened that the first act of the Congress on September 7, 1774, was a prayer, pronounced by an Episcopalian clergyman dressed in his pontificals. And what did he read? He read a Jewish prayer, Psalm 35 in the Book of Common Prayer. Now imagine the king's troops moving against the homes of some of the people gathered there. Imagine the delegates from South Carolina and New York thinking that the fleet might be shelling their homes soon.

"Plead my cause, O Lord, with them that strive with me. Fight against them that fight against me.
Take hold of buckler and shield, and rise up for my help.
...Say to my soul, "I am your salvation."
Let those be ashamed and dishonored who seek my life. Let those be turned back and humiliated who devise evil against me."

Before the Reverend Duché knelt Washington, Henry, Randolph, Rutledge, Lee, and Jay; and by their side, with heads bowed, the Puritan patriots who could imagine at that moment their own homes being bombarded and overrun. Over these bowed heads the Reverend Duché uttered what all testified was an eloquent prayer for America, for Congress, for the Province of Massachusetts Bay, and especially for the town of Boston. The emotion in the room was palpable, and John Adams wrote to Abigail that night that he had never heard a better prayer or one so well pronounced. "I never saw a greater effect upon an audience. It seemed as if heaven had ordained that that Psalm be read on that morning. It was enough to melt a stone. I saw tears gush into the eyes of the old, grave pacific Quakers of Philadelphia. I must beg you, Abigail, to read that Psalm."

In this fashion, right at its beginning, this nation formed a covenant with God which is repeated in the Declaration: "with a firm reliance on the protection of

Divine Providence." The founders pledged their fidelity to the will of God, and asked God to protect their liberty. They further enacted this covenant in many later acts of Congress regarding Days of Fasting. Within the first six months, for instance, Congress put out a proclamation that every American state set aside a day of prayer and fasting:

> "December 11, 1776: RESOLVED that it be recommended to all the United States as soon as possible to appoint a day of solemn fasting and humiliation to implore the Almighty God to forgiveness of the many sins prevailing among all ranks and to beg the countenance and the assistance of his Providence in the prosecution of the present just and necessary war."

And then, within another year, an act of Congress instituted a Day of Thanksgiving to commemorate the signal successes of that year, and again the next year. Years later, in *The Federalist* No. 38, Publius marveled at the improbable unanimity achieved among fragmented delegates, from free states and slave, from small states and large, from rich states and poor. "It is impossible for the man of pious reflection not to perceive in it a finger of the Almighty hand which has been so frequently and signally extended to our relief in the critical stages of the revolution." Three times *The Federalist* notes the blessings of Providence upon this country.

An Act of Providence

On the night before the battle of Long Island, the Americans received intelligence that the British were attacking the next morning, and Washington was trapped with his whole army. Washington saw that there was only one way out – by boat. During the night, the Americans gathered as many boats as they could. There weren't enough. Morning came, and more than half the army was still on shore. A huge fog rolled in and covered them till noon. They escaped, and when the British closed the trap, there was no one there. The Americans interpreted that fog as an act of Providence.

In the preaching of the time, Americans learned as follows: Providence does not mean that God works magically; rather, from all time every detail of the tapestry is known to the one who weaves it. To the Eternal God, there is neither time nor sequence, but every detail of the tapestry is visible to Him as if in one simultaneous moment, each thing acting independently and freely, but cohering as a whole, like characters in a well-wrought novel. Thus, the rival general, on the morning of the great battle comes down with dysentery and can't concentrate. Nothing more common in the affairs of human beings than circumstance and chance, which only those who lived through them in time and sequence found to be surprising. The very sermon Witherspoon preached on behalf of independence in April 1776 was a sermon on how Providence acts by contingent and indirect actions – not *fore*seen, because God doesn't "foresee" anything. He's *present* to everything, in the Jewish and Christian understanding. He's not *before* or *after*, He's present to all things at one time. And like a great novelist, He sees the details of what He does, and how they all hook together, without forcing anybody's liberty, without manipulating anything.

The Author of Liberty

When Jefferson wrote the Declaration of Independence, he mentioned God twice. Before the Congress would sign it, members insisted on two more references to God. Thus, the four names already mentioned: the *Author* of nature and nature's laws; the *Creator* who endowed in us our rights; the *Judge* to whom we appeal in witness that our motives spring not out of seditiousness, but from a dear love of liberty, and a deep sense of our own proper dignity; and a trust in *Divine Providence*.

The fundamental meaning of the Jewish, and later the Christian, Bible is that the axis of the universe is what happens in the interior of the human being. Every story in the Bible is a story of what happens in the arena of the human will. In one chapter King David is faithful to his Lord and in the next, not. And the suspense of every chapter is: What will humans choose next? Liberty is the reason God made the universe. He wanted somewhere one creature capable of recognizing that He had made all things, that the creation is good, and that He had extended his hand in friendship. He wanted at least one creature to be able, not as a slave but as a free woman or a free man, to reciprocate his proffered friendship. That, in a nutshell, is what Judaism is, and what Christianity is. (Christianity, of course, played an historical role in making the God of Judaism known universally.)

The members of Congress on July 2, 1776, were about to make themselves liable to the charge of treason and to humiliate their children into the nth generation for being the descendants of traitors. They needed that reference to their *Judge* in the Declaration. And they wanted that reference to *Providence*, to declare that God is on the side of Liberty, and those who trust in liberty will therefore prevail. Whatever the odds, Providence will see to it that they prevail.

Let me recall, from one of the old American hymns, words that reflect exactly this biblical vision. This world didn't just "happen," it was created. It was created for a purpose, and that purpose is *liberty:*

> "Our fathers God! To Thee,
> Author of liberty,
> To Thee we sing.
> Long may our land be bright
> With freedom's holy light;
> Protect us by Thy might,
> Great God our king."

A typical sentiment of the American people then, and even now.

I've mentioned that though some historians say they were deists, the early Americans who believed that the lifting of the fog on Long Island was an act of God, were not deists. Their god was not a "watchmaker God," who winds the universe up and lets it go. Their god was a God who cares about contingent affairs, loves particular nations, is interested in particular peoples and particular circumstances. Their god was the God of Judaism, the God of Providence. Not a swallow falls in the field but this God knows of it. His action is in the details.

The Logic of Faith

The Third Article of the Constitution of Massachusetts:

> "As the happiness of a people and the good order and preservation of civil government essentially depend upon piety, religion, and morality, and as these cannot be generally diffused through a community but by the institution of the public worship of God and of public instructions in piety, religion, and morality: Therefore, To promote their happiness and to secure the good order and preservation of their government, the people of this commonwealth have a right to invest their legislature with power to authorize and require, and the legislature shall, from time to time, authorize and require, the several towns, par-

ishes, precincts, and other bodies-politic or religious societies to make suitable provision, at
their own expense, for the institution of the
public worship of God and for the support
and maintenance of public Protestant teachers
of piety, religion, and morality in all cases
where such provision shall not be made voluntarily."

When this article was attacked as an infringement
on religious liberty, John Adams replied, in effect,
"Not at all, you don't have to believe it. But if you
want the good order that comes from instruction in
religion, particularly the Jewish and Christian religion,
then you have to pay for it." That's not the way we
think today, I hastily add, but this is the sort of logic
our founders used. Let us walk through the three cru-
cial steps of this logic, one by one.

Right at the beginning of *The Federalist*, in the
second paragraph, the author says this generation of
Americans is called upon to decide for all time
whether governments can be formed "through reflection and choice" or must "forever be formed through
accident and force." That's what the Americans were
called upon to decide: whether a government may be
formed through *reflection* and *choice*.

They then faced the question: How do you insti-
tutionalize such a decision? By calling a Constitutional
Convention and then having the agreed-upon text
ratified in a manner that permits the whole people to

participate in the decision. Can there be enough votes for something like that? Can people put aside their regional prejudices? Can they put aside their personal ambitions? Can they think about what's good for the long run? For posterity? That's what *The Federalist* tries to elicit -- a long-range view, not what people feel at the moment.

Remember the ambitions of that moment. Many New Yorkers wanted New York to be a separate nation. (The early maps of New York go all the way out to the Pacific Ocean-it's not called "the Empire State" for nothing.) If New York becomes a separate state, it will have its own secretary of state, its own commander in chief, its own secretary of the treasury; distinguished families in New York will become ambassadors to the Court of St. James and to Paris and so forth. Such a dream might seem very attractive to some leading families, but would it be good for the country? If New York were to vote to become an independent nation, there could be no union between New England and the South. *Reflection* and *choice* were, then, the hinges of liberty. What Americans *meant* by liberty are those acts that are made from reflection and choice. The acts that we commit ourselves to when we have reflected on the alternatives and when we understand the consequences. That's freedom.

What you do by impulse, by contrast, is not freedom; that's slavery to your impulses. Such slavery is what the animals live under. They're hungry; they need to eat. That's not freedom; it's animal instinct.

Freedom is not doing what you want to do; freedom is doing what, after reflection, you know you *ought* to do. That's what freedom is, and that's why early American thought has been summed up thus: "Confirm thy soul in self-control, Thy liberty in law." Freedom springs from self-government, after reflection and calm deliberate choice.

The second step in the argument is this: To have reflection and choice, you need people with enough virtue to have command of their passions. You need people, that is, with the habits that allow them to reflect, to take time to be dispassionate, to see consequences clearly, and then to make a choice based upon commitment. None of us act that way all the time. But we do aspire to have at least sufficient virtue to live responsibly. For how can a people unable to govern their passions in their private lives possibly be able to practice self-government in their public lives? It doesn't compute. In short, freedom in a republic is not feasible without virtue in a republic.

Next, the third step. George Washington said in his Farewell Address that most people are not going to have virtue or good habits in the long run without religion. And what he meant by that can be recited very simply. As Jews and Christians understand it, religion is not just a cold law; it is a relationship with a person. A person who knows even your secret thoughts. So religion adds a personal motive to the idea of virtue. In addition to that, this Judge sees you even when you're alone, even when you're in secret, even when the doors are closed. This is a Judge who knows whether or not you paint the bottom of the chair. Republics depend on virtue that holds up under such tests. The founding generation used the example of the well-known doctor in Massachusetts who, having been involved in adultery, turned out also to be a British spy. This was a lesson they often referred to. A man who thinks he can get away with things in secret is not reliable for a republic. A republic cannot be made up of people who think they can do in secret what they wouldn't do in public. Jefferson wrote a very touching letter to this effect.

This is why the founders thought that whatever may be said of persons of "peculiar character," as Washington said (some scholars think he's referring to Jefferson), we must not believe that virtue can be maintained in the long run without religion. Our sons are going to forget about the Revolution, the founders expected; they're going to forget the suffering we went through. They're going to forget the frozen feet at Valley Forge and the gangrene and the hunger, the lack of pay and the despair. They're going to forget all that, and their grandchildren are going to be tired of hearing it. There's a moral entropy in human affairs, such that even if one generation succeeds in reaching a very high moral level, it's almost impossible for the next generation and the one after that to maintain it. A republic, therefore, has to fight moral entropy. That's why there will have to be a series of moral awakenings. The founders didn't see how that would happen without religious inspiration, beyond a merely utilitarian impulse.

So there are three principles in this fundamental logic: *No republic without liberty; no liberty without virtue; no virtue without religion.* Now, doesn't that sound old-fashioned? In these days, doesn't it sound hardly tenable? Yet our founders were right. Is not our present circumstance dangerous to the Republic?

The Choice of Liberty

I first heard this story alluded to in Ronald Reagan's Inaugural Address. Dr. Joseph Warren, the family doctor of Abigail and John Adams in Boston, was among the first to join the Sons of Liberty and to stand with the men at Lexington. In fact, he was an officer, and he took a bullet through his hair right above his ear, where it left a crease, but he stood his ground. Two months later, Dr. Warren was commissioned as a major general of the Continental Army. It was a great title, but there wasn't much of an army for the defense of Boston, toward which the British fleet was bringing reinforcements. Dr. Warren learned just four days after he was commissioned that that night the Americans had sent 1,500 men up Bunker Hill. It was one of those still nights when hardly a sound traveled out over the water, where the British fleet was anchored. In the stillness, the troops dug, muffling their shovels, and constructed wooden fortifications, being careful not to strike anything with an axe.

In the morning, the British on board ship awakened to find that Bunker Hill was fortified, and began a five-hour bombardment. Warren heard the bombardment as he was on horseback riding toward Boston, and arrived at Bunker Hill by a back route and managed to climb up into the ranks. He didn't try to take command; he just went into the ranks, in the front rows.

After the bombardment, some of the British soldiers came on land and put Charlestown to the torch, and tongues of flame from 500 homes, businesses, and churches leapt into the sky. Everything in Charlestown burned. Breathless, Abigail Adams watched from a hilltop to the south. She heard the cannons from the warships bombarding Bunker Hill for five long hours as Joseph Warren rode to his position. The American irregulars proved their discipline that day and the accuracy of huntsmen firing in concentrated bursts. They had only four or five rounds apiece. Twice they broke the forward march of thirty-five hundred British troops with fire so withering they blew away as many as 70 to 90 percent of the foremost companies of Redcoats, who lost that day more than a thousand dead.

Then the ammunition of the Americans ran out. While the bulk of the Continental Army retreated, the last units stayed in their trenches to hold off the British hand-to-hand. That is where Major General Joseph Warren was last seen fighting until a close-range bullet felled him. The British officers had him decapitated and bore his head aloft to General Gage.

Freedom is always the most precarious regime. Even a single generation can throw it all away. Every generation must reflect and must choose. Joseph Warren had earlier told the men of Massachusetts at Lexington:

> *Our country is in danger now, but not to be despaired of. On you depend the fortunes of America. You are to decide the important questions upon which rest the happiness and the liberty of millions not yet born. Act worthy of yourselves.*

- November 9, 2001

MICHAEL NOVAK, *retired George Frederick Jewett Scholar in Religion, Philosophy and Public Policy from the American Enterprise Institute, is an author, philosopher, and theologian. Novak's whole life has been a story of religious scholarship, social commentary and intellectual independence. His insights into the spiritual foundations of economic and political systems and his articulation of the moral ideals of democratic capitalism have secured his place as an original thinker of the late 20th and early 21st centuries.*

Mr. Novak is the author or editor of more than 45 books from 1961 until the present, including two novels and one book of verse. His books have been translated into every major Western language, as well as Bengali, Korean, Chinese, and Japanese.

The presidents of three nations – the Czech Republic, Poland and Slovakia – have given Michael Novak the highest award they can bestow on a foreign citizen. Each cited Novak's work as human rights ambassador under Ronald Reagan, his 11 years of service on the boards of Radio Free Europe and Radio Liberty, and the pre-1989 influence of his book, The Spirit of Democratic Capitalism (1982), translated and distributed by underground presses behind the Iron Curtain in the 1980s. As one reviewer said of that volume, it "may prove one of those rare books that actually changes the way things are."

Novak has been granted 26 honorary degrees (including four in Latin America and three in Europe), the Friend of Freedom Award from the Coalition for a Democratic Majority, the George Washington Honor Medal from the Freedom Foundation, and the Ellis Island Medal of Honor, among numerous other honors. His selection as recipient of the 1994 Templeton

Templeton Prize for Progress in Religion capped a career of leadership in theological and philosophical discourse.

Novak has taught at Harvard, Stanford, SUNY Old Westbury, Syracuse and Notre Dame. Since 2010 Novak's home base during the academic year has been southwest Florida, where he continues writing and teaching at Ave Maria University.

2

The Late Cardinal
Avery Dulles, S. J.
on
Faith and Civility

"Quite apart from its consequences in the political order, this substitution of mere politeness for genuine civility makes a negative impact on the faith of every religious group."

At St. Charles, I am told Latin is a required subject. Having had a reasonably good education in that language myself, I can say that I have found it a great help not only in my work as a priest but in many other aspects of life. It helps one to learn many modern languages and to speak and write correct English. For example, it is helpful to know that the word "civility" in the title of this lecture comes from the Latin word *civilitas*. It means the quality of a citizen, *civis*, or that which is befitting of the citizen. The citizen is contrasted with the slave and the barbarian.

The slave, being denied the privileges attractive

to membership, is in the society but not of it. According to the ancient theory, slaves were inferior persons, incapable of rising to the exigencies of citizenship. They were supposed to lack the intelligence and education needed to guide their lives by reason and enter into relationships with others on the basis of rational discourse. Incapable of acting voluntarily for the general good, they had to be commanded and, if necessary, coerced.

"Barbarian" is another word taken into English from Latin. The Latin term *barbarus* means simply a foreigner. In classical antiquity, people who lived outside the Greco-Roman world were considered wild and uncultivated. Hence the words "barbarian" and "barbaric" took on the secondary meaning of savage or uncouth. Like slaves, barbarians were beyond the ambit of civilized humanity. They gathered at the city gates, always threatening to invade. Just as the slave had to be coerced, the barbarian had to be resisted. Neither, by definition, was capable of rising to the standard of rationally ordered cultural development. Citizens were expected to treat one another civilly - that is to say, as intelligent beings who could freely respond to reasons, once these were shown. No one is born with all the qualities required for civility. We all have to be educated so that we can deal and be dealt with according to the standards and disciplines of citizenship.

Civilization, once achieved, does not automatically perpetuate itself. We are always at the brink of a precipice, in imminent danger of relapsing into barbarism. As Father John Courtney Murray wrote more than 40 years ago:

"Society becomes barbarian when men are huddled together under the rule of force or fear; when economic interests assume the primacy over higher values; when material standards of mass and quantity crush out the values of quality and excellence; when technology assumes an autonomous existence and embarks on a course of unlimited self-exploitation without purposeful guidance from the higher disciples of politics and morals (one thinks of Cape Canaveral); ... when the ways of men come under the sway of the instinctual, the impulsive, the compulsive."

Since the time that Father Murray wrote these words, the Western world, including the United States, seems to be careening down the path toward a new age of barbarism, this time brought on from inside rather than from outside. The barbarian is often within the gates, highly placed in the worlds of business or finance. Our world is increasingly dominated by the rules of the market. The market is driven by the media of communication, the media of communication by advertising, and advertising by catering to the basest human instincts. Everything seems to be geared toward satisfying the urges for entertainment, excitement and instant gratification. Anyone who seeks to rise above the general level of mediocrity is tarred with the accusation of elitism.

The trend toward barbarity is accelerated by aggression or terrorism from outside the society. In the face of real and imagined threats, civil liberties are curbed and people are treated without due respect for their freedom and rationality. In times of national emergency, fear and force become the principal determinants of behavior. Another factor militating against civility is the increasing pluralism of our society. Pluralism is frequently promoted on the ground that every group should be encouraged to cultivate its own traditions and values. But a society is by definition an association of people who have a common goal. Unless we have some common convictions about reality and some common standards of decency, we cannot agree on what is right and wrong, what is permitted and what is forbidden, what is desirable and what is to be avoided.

When common standards are lacking, dialogue breaks down. People cannot reason with one another because they have no common premises and no shared universe of discourse. How can I reason with another person about what ought to be believed and done unless we have some common starting point and principles of argument? How can I talk about literature with someone who is illiterate? How can I converse about ethics with someone who has no sense of right and wrong? I can fruitfully discuss religious questions with parties who accept the existence of God as known through the Bible and the Church, but otherwise it may be hard to find agreed sources and norms. And so likewise, if two of us have radically disparate political philosophies, we are in no position to debate about the merits of different candidates and platforms.

Pluralism, therefore, is not an unqualified good. Unless a consensus can be achieved regarding the principles that sustain civility, dialogue breaks down. The member groups are spiritual aliens if not enemies to one another. Instead of reasoning together they berate each other. Passion and prejudice take the place of reasoned discourse. Personal invective and defamation of character intrude upon logic. It is a constant struggle to achieve the civility required to sustain a well-functioning republic.

Civility and Religion

As a theologian, I should like to offer a few thoughts on the relationship between civility and religion. Civility can, I suppose, exist without religion. In Greece and Rome it was only tenuously connected with religion. But where a religious faith such as Christianity is seeking to gain a hearing it can profit from an environment of civility. Such an environment provides heralds of the faith with an opportunity to present their case, provided that they are able to propose their message in a rationally credible form. Faith in the Christian sense of the word is, of course, a response to revelation. Although it is not a deliverance of reason, it is in accord with everything that reason can establish.

Ever since St. Paul's sermon to the Athenians at the Areopagus, Christianity has learned how to appeal to the reason of those who are ready to listen and make them at least give serious consideration to its claims. In a barbaric community, by contrast, the voice of reason cannot assert itself. More often than not, heralds of the faith are banished or brutally persecuted because they are perceived as hostile to the entrenched ideas and customs of the people. Freedom of religion is closely connected with civility.

Christian faith and civility have been allied from the beginning. Jesus himself, as we know him from the Gospels, never uses or encourages physical violence. When his followers want to acclaim him as a temporal king he resists them, insisting that his sovereignty is purely spiritual. Bearing witness to the truth, he asks for a free assent of faith. He invites a discipleship that is free and uncoerced. Extolling love toward enemies, he counsels nonresistance to evil and patience under suffering. He urges his disciples to propagate the gospel by bearing witness to his word and drawing others by the cords of reason, truth and love.

Paul, the Apostle best known to us because of his many writings, never mentions civility as a Christian virtue, but the idea appears in equivalent terms in his letters. He exhorts the Galatians to exhibit joy, peace, patience, and kindness, and to avoid strife, jealousy, anger, and the like (Gal 5:19-23). In his celebrated hymn to charity in the 13th chapter of First Corinthians, he insists on the indispensability of love. Love, he writes, "is patient and kind; love is not jealous or boastful; it is not arrogant or rude. Love does not insist on its own way; it is not irritable or resentful; it does not rejoice at wrong but rejoices in the right" (1 Cor 13:4-6). Although Christian love vastly excels over civil friendship, it fulfills in an eminent way the requirements of civility. Just as civility is the precondition for a well-functioning commonwealth, so charity sustains appropriate human relationships in the Church as the Body of Christ. United in spirit, Christians are to treat one another with mutual respect, kindness and consideration. Going beyond the classical descriptions of civil society, Paul emphasizes generosity to the poor and consideration for the weak (cf. 1 Cor 8:4-13).

Paul did not directly attack the institution of slavery, which was simply taken for granted in the world of his day. But he exhorts his friend Philemon to welcome back his slave Onesimus, who has become a Christian, not simply as a slave but as a beloved brother in Christ. Christian charity, then, overcame the kind of chattel slavery prevalent in the ancient world.

In the early centuries, Christianity achieved sophisticated formulations of its ethical teaching with the help of Greek philosophers especially Plato, Aristotle and the Stoics. The Fathers of the Church assimilated the finest fruits of Greek and Roman philosophy, literature and jurisprudence. When the Empire was overrun by barbarians, the Church preserved the monuments of civilization in her monasteries, so that in the ensuing centuries, she could pass them on to new populations. The monastic and cathedral schools of the Middle Ages were the chief instruments for taming the barbarians and building a new Christian civilization.

Although we have every right to admire the achievements of medieval Christianity in the fields of philosophy and theology, arts and literature, it must be acknowledged that medieval civilization was in some respects still backward. Traces of barbarism remained. Oppression and violence retained their grip on society, as the sad history of persecutions, crusades and inquisitions attests. Force and fear, rather than reason and persuasion, were often used to secure conformity to law and religious orthodoxy. The vast majority of the people still languished in ignorance and servitude.

A major breakthrough in the history of freedom occurred with the United States Declaration of Independence, the Constitution and the Bill of Rights. The American experiment in ordered liberty was a perilous venture. For its success it depended upon a virtuous citizenry who were schooled in the disciplines of civility. The people had to embrace the common ideals embodied in the founding documents, holding a certain body of truths as evident beyond dispute □ most centrally, that all human beings are created by God with certain inalienable rights. These convictions sustain the American experiment

The Declaration on Religious Freedom, adopted by the Second Vatican Council in 1965, may be seen as a religious counterpart to the founding documents of the American republic. In this Declaration the Catholic Church formally signified her acceptance of the principles of the free society. Without any minimizing of the claims of the Catholic Church to be the true Church of Christ and the sacrament of his saving presence in the world, the Declaration calls upon Catholics to accept the principles of a civil society that is not dominated by any one religion and to cultivate civil relationships with persons who do not share the Church's faith.

The Declaration on Religious Freedom lays down principles bearing on what I have been calling civility. It begins with these words:

> "A sense of the dignity of the human person has been impressing itself more and more deeply on the consciousness of contemporary man. And the demand is increasingly made that men should act on their own judgment, enjoying and making use of a responsible freedom, not driven by coercion but motivated by a sense of duty. The demand is also made that constitutional limits should be set to the powers of government in order that there may be no encroachment on the rightful freedom of the person and of association."

The Declaration goes on to say that one of the principal requirements of the human spirit is the free exercise of religion. In the terms of this paper, I might say that civility requires leaving people civilly free to seek or not to seek the truth of religion. Coercion in this area is viewed as barbaric.

Although the Declaration on Religious Freedom was written with special attention to the relations among Christians of different ecclesial allegiances, its principles apply likewise to relations between different religious faiths.

Contemporary Tensions and Proposals

In the years since Vatican II, the various religions of the world have been thrust into much closer contact with one another than ever before. Reciprocal relations among Christians, Jews, Muslims, Buddhists and Hindus are a matter of daily concern, not only in foreign affairs but to some extent within our national borders. It is not at all clear that all these groups, with their different norms of truth and scales of values, can be conjoined in a single society. Under what conditions can they treat one another as civilized persons rather than barbarians? As we know from current events in the Holy Land, India, Indonesia, Nigeria and elsewhere, adherents of different religions are prone to engage in violence. When there are sharp religious differences within a single society, violence is hard to avoid.

One proposal for escaping the tensions among religious groups is secularism, a system that has prevailed with fair success in the politics of Turkey, less consistently in India, and to a modest degree in countries like our own. The secular thesis is that religion is a divisive force. To keep it under control, religion should be banished from public life and allowed to function only in the strictly private sphere. This solution, sweepingly applied, is unworthy of the free society. It is incompatible with the public documents previously cited, in which the United States is described as one nation under God, the creator of all human beings. On all our currency, we inscribe the motto, "In God we trust." Religion plays a prominent place in many aspects of our public life.

All the great religions have teachings which, if true, should have a beneficial impact on society. The Catholic faith, for example, has much to say about topics such as education, healthcare, the economy, crime and punishment, war and peace. To maintain, as Marxists do, that religions may not function except as private associations, conducting worship services for their own members, is an affront to religious freedom. Civility demands that believers should be accorded full freedom to express their perspective on issues of public concern.

A second proposal for resolving the tension is less overtly hostile to religion but in the long run more insidious. John Murray Cuddihy calls it "civil religion," or alternatively, "the religion of civility."

The phenomenon is pervasive in contemporary America. The various religions, Cuddihy contends, have been tamed into denominations. Dropping their exclusive claims, they lower themselves to the status of voluntary associations of likeminded individuals. Becoming diffident in expressing their religious identity, people get into the habit of saying no longer "I am Catholic (or Jewish, or Protestant or whatever)," but "I happen to be Catholic" or even "I was raised Catholic." Citizens are under constant pressure to profess an equal respect for every religion. Cuddihy traces how the old formula "outside the Church no salvation" has been reinterpreted so as to become virtually meaningless. Religion in the United States, he contends, continues to function only within the boundaries permitted by the code of what he calls civility.

To illustrate the mentality of civil religion, Cuddihy tells a touching story of about the Lutheran pastor Dietrich Bonhoeffer, when he was at the point of being executed by the Nazis in 1945. "Called to conduct his last worship service in prison shortly before his execution ... [Bonhoeffer] held back, for he did not want to offend his neighbor, a Soviet officer." Commenting on this event, Cuddihy remarks: "A new offense has swallowed up the ancient skandalon; the rites of faith perform themselves in the rites of love; the *ius divinum* self-destructs: a new *ius civile* is all in all."

The Debasing of Civility

The term "civility" has taken on a new meaning. Whereas in the classical sense it had been the socio-cultural framework that makes serious argument possible, it has now become a barrier against argument. To be civil, in the popular estimation, is to avoid giving any offense; it is to refrain from challenging others on the ground that doing so might make them feel uncomfortable. Not infrequently today, people claim to be offended if we simply manifest our beliefs. They make us feel guilty because we hold a position different from theirs. A wall of politeness prevents the question of truth about religious questions from ever being raised.

John Courtney Murray, in the book already referred to, analyzed the causes for this debasing of civility. In a situation of unreconciled pluralism, he says, ideological divisions make honest dialogue and argument exceedingly difficult. Seeking to avoid insult and violence, Americans put on the mask of polite urbanity, ceasing to challenge one another. Civic amity of this kind is not real friendship, but a code of conduct that conceals the wars still being waged beneath the surface.

The shift in the meaning of civility is doing serious harm. As one nation under God, Americans are, in Lincoln's famous phrase, "dedicated to the proposition that all men are created equal." If the tenet that all men are created by God with certain inalienable rights is no longer held to be true, the foundations of civility are undermined, and the American experiment in ordered liberty begins to totter. If we lose sight of the transcendent ground, our human rights have no solid anchorage that prevents them from being voted out of existence. Pope John Paul II has clearly traced the process by which relativism and agnosticism eat away at the structures of authentic democracy. In his great encyclical, *Centesimus annus*, he writes:

"Nowadays there is a tendency to claim that agnosticism and skeptical relativism are the philosophy and the basic attitude which correspond to democratic forms of political life. Those who are convinced that they know the truth and firmly adhere to it are considered unreliable from a democratic point of view, since they do not accept the idea that truth is determined by the majority, or that it is subject to variation according to different political tends. It must be observed in this regard that if there is no ultimate truth to guide and direct political activity, then ideas and convictions can easily be manipulated for reasons of power. As history demonstrates, a democracy without values easily turns into open or thinly disguised totalitarianism."

When he wrote these words the Pope may have

been recalling that Hitler himself came into power by popular election.

Quite apart from its consequences in the political order, this substitution of mere politeness for genuine civility makes a negative impact on the faith of every religious group. It deters believers from giving expression to their real convictions and bearing witness to the truths they hold. Dialogue with persons who do not share our faith ceases to be a serious common quest for truth and becomes an exercise in discovering ways of masking real differences and forging a merely pragmatic consensus. The Catholic, the Jew, the Protestant and others begin to feel embarrassed about what is distinctive to their specific religion, as though it were an ugly secret.

What Is and Is Not Offensive

There is of course a proper place for politeness and decorum. In the November 2002 issue of the New Oxford Review, Alice von Hildebrand has a fine article on "What's 'Offensive' and What's Not." It is unacceptable, she says, to try to wound others, and to scoff at their beliefs. The Catholic League, headed by William Donohue, has every right to denounce those who make Catholic beliefs and practices the butt of their scorn. Hatred and contempt for religious groups should be opposed not because such attitudes offend people's feelings but because they are morally wrong.

Inoffensiveness is carried to excess when people regard any manifestation of one's beliefs as objectionable, as we already noticed in the pathetic case of Bonhoeffer's final hour. Increasingly we find that a new pattern of behavior is being socially, if not legally, imposed. A handful of people can prevent major segments of the population from giving public expression to their religious beliefs on the ground that they consider it "offensive." Believers may not pray in public, or if they are allowed to do so, they may not indicate to whom they are praying. William Donohue reports that in King County, Washington, employees can be arrested for saying "Merry Christmas" because it is regarded as offensive to non-Christians. To be "politically correct" and sensitive to others, one must say, "happy holidays." In the name of this new ideology, efforts are being made to discard the firm professions of faith in God in the Declaration of Independence and in the Gettysburg Address. Last June an appellate court declared the Pledge of Allegiance to the U. S. flag unconstitutional in public schools because it includes the words "under God." Public displays of crèches and menorahs are at times forbidden. If we continue to drift in this direction, I submit the foundations of our republic will be gravely weakened clearing the way for tyranny.

The true concept of civility would give different groups in society full freedom to express and propagate their beliefs, even in the public forum, provided that they are not misrepresenting or ridiculing the beliefs of others or threatening just public order. Others have no right to take offense when I express my faith, nor do I have any right to take offense when they express theirs.

Reversion Toward Stridency

The excesses of the movement toward superficial and false politeness, with the consequent limits on the free exercise of religion, can be breeding grounds for a new barbarism. Frustrated by the restrictions, devout believers relapse into polemics. As an example one could mention the developments at St. Benedict Center near Harvard Square, which began in 1946 to publish a journal called From the Housetops. Explaining the title, Mrs. Catherine Clarke, the principal founder of the Center, declared:

> "The full, unequivocal, uncompromised message of Jesus Christ had to be thundered to the world again. It could not merely be told. It had to be shouted, bellowed, because the world was deaf, asleep, already half-dead. Polite talking would not wake it nor would vague reference, large gesture, platitudinous utterance. "Never give offense" seemed to be the Catholic policy of the day. We knew it was impossible to tell the truth and not to give offense."

As some of you may know, St. Benedict Center went to such extremes in its vehemence that it had to be placed under interdict and its spiritual leader, Father Leonard Feeney, excommunicated for more than 20 years. Their "barbarism" was no more acceptable than the "civility" they repudiated.

Somewhat different is the case of the celebrated French philosopher, Jacques Maritain. An adult convert to the faith, he spent much of his life skating on the fine line between polemics and civility. In an early book on the Jewish philosopher Henri Bergson, he made some bitter observations about his Catholic philosopher colleagues, accusing them of denying to the public the word of life which alone counts for ultimate salvation. "If they have such words," he asked "why do they not cry them from the housetops, asking their disciples to give, if necessary, their very blood for them?"

In mid-life, Maritain worked for many years at the Center for Advanced Study at Princeton and became much more discreet in his utterances. At one point he found himself accused of diluting Catholic doctrine by the outspoken director of the Aquinas Center at Princeton, Father Hugh Halton, O.P., who adopted a stance similar to Feeney's.

Toward the end of his life Maritain retired to France, where he resumed the more aggressive language of his early years. Shortly after the Second Vatican Council he published a book with the significant title "The Peasant of the Garonne: An Old Layman

Questions Himself about the Present Time." No longer wearing the mantle of the sophisticated philosopher, he resolved to speak with the bluntness of a peasant or, we might say, a barbarian. In Maritain's own words. a peasant is "a man who puts his foot in his mouth, or who calls a spade a spade." The peasant has no standards of politeness to keep him from upsetting the applecart. There is some irony in Maritain's title. A philosopher of exquisite urbanity, he could not possibly write as a peasant. But he rightly judges that the intellectual elite would consider him boorish for challenging the dogmas of the day - historical relativism, the myth of inevitable progress, and the supposedly unqualified blessings of technocracy. He intended to deliver these challenges in unmistakable terms.

Cuddihy draws the conclusion: "The Church will not survive without a willingness to be uncouth. In the end, truth is an incivil thing." But this is not a fair description of Maritain's position. He never adopted the stridency of Catherine Clarke, Leonard Feeney or Hugh Halton. While forthrightly denouncing what he saw as error, he preserved the virtue of civility, properly so called. Like Father Murray, he spoke in measured tones, giving reasons for his views and avoiding malicious defamation. Together with John Courtney Murray, Jacques Maritain stands as a model of how to combine true civility with intrepid witness to the faith.

Conclusion

I conclude, contrary to Cudihy, that truth is not uncivil. In a pluralist society, civility can forge bonds of union. It can support honest dialogue and prevent controversy from degenerating into slander. But civility should not be equated with timidity or evasion of the issues. Far from preventing argument civility makes argument possible. It appeals to reason and free consent. Schools such as St. Charles can perform a great service if they instill into their students the ability to think clearly and to give a persuasive account of the hope that is in them. Their graduates will know how to combine good citizenship with loyal commitment to their religious faith.

- January 8, 2003

AVERY CARDINAL DULLES, S.J. *(August 24, 1918-December 12, 2008) was the Laurence J. McGinley Professor of Religion and Society at Fordham University, a position he had held since 1988. An internationally known author and lecturer, he was born in Auburn, New York, on August 24, 1918, the son of John Foster Dulles and Janet Pomeroy Avery Dulles. He received his primary school education in New York City, and attended secondary schools in Switzerland and New England. After graduating from Harvard College in 1940, he spent a year and a half in Harvard Law School before serving in the United States Navy, emerging with the rank of lieutenant.*

Upon his discharge from the Navy in 1946, Avery Dulles entered the Jesuit Order, and was ordained to the priesthood in 1956. After a year in Germany, he studied at the Gregorian University in Rome, and was awarded the doctorate in Sacred Theology in 1960. He was created a Cardinal of the Catholic Church in Rome on February 21, 2001 by Pope John Paul II, the first American-born theologian who is not a bishop to receive this honor.   Avery Cardinal Dulles died peacefully in the Lord on December 12, 2008, at the Jesuit Infirmary at Murray-Weigel Hall on the campus of Fordham University.

Cardinal Dulles served on the faculty of Woodstock College from 1960 to 1974, and of The Catholic University of America from 1974 to 1988. He was a visiting professor at: The Gregorian University (Rome), Weston School of Theology, Union Theological Seminary (New York, N.Y.), Princeton Theological Seminary, Episcopal Seminary (Alexandria, Va.), Lutheran Theological Seminary (Gettysburg, Pa.), Boston Col-

lege, Campion Hall (Oxford University), the University of Notre Dame, the Catholic University at Leuven, Yale University, and St. Joseph's Seminary, Dunwoodie.

The author of more than 750 articles on theological topics, Cardinal Dulles published 23 books, including Models of the Church (1974), Models of Revelation (1983), The Catholicity of the Church (1985), The Craft of Theology: From Symbol to System (1992), The Assurance of Things Hoped For: A Theology of Christian Faith (1994), The Splendor of Faith: The Theological Vision of Pope John Paul II (1999; revised in 2003 for the 25th anniversary of the papal election), and The New World of Faith (2000), Newman (2002). His latest book are a revised edition of The History of Apologetics, (revised edition, 2005), and Magisterium: Teacher and Guardian of the Faith (2007). The 50th anniversary edition of his book, A Testimonial to Grace, the account of his conversion to Catholicism, was republished in 1996 by the original publishers, Sheed and Ward, with an afterword containing his reflections on the 50 years since he became a Catholic.

Past President of both the Catholic Theological Society of America and the American Theological Society and Professor Emeritus at The Catholic University of America, Cardinal Dulles served on the International Theological Commission and as a member of the United States Lutheran/Roman Catholic Dialogue. He was a consultant to the Committee on Doctrine of the National Conference of Catholic Bishops. He possessed an impressive collection of awards, including Phi Beta Kappa, the Croix de Guerre, the Cardinal Spellman Award for distinguished achievement in theology, the Boston College Presidential Bicentennial Award, the Christus Magister Medal from the

University of Portland (Oregon), the Religious Education Forum Award from the National Catholic Educational Association, America Magazine's Campion Award, the F. Sadlier Dinger Award for contributions to the catechetical ministry of the Church, the Cardinal Gibbons Award from The Catholic University of America, the John Carroll Society Medal, the Jerome Award from the Catholic Library Association of America, Fordham's Founders Award, Gaudium Award from the Breukelein Institute, the Newman Award from Loyola College in Baltimore, the Marianist Award from the University of Dayton, the Saint Thomas Aquinas Medallion from Thomas Aquinas College in California, St. Joseph's Seminary Dunwoodie Annual Dinner Award, the President's Medal from Canisius College in Buffalo, the Loyola medal from Seattle University, and 38 honorary doctorates.

3

Joel. I Klein

on

American Education and a Call to Public Service

"Our union is not only not imperfect, but it is far from perfect, and it will never become all of the things that we hope unless each future generation of leaders is prepared to commit itself..."

I know we have many distinguished people here in the audience and for fear of insulting some, I won't mention any, but in a real sense each of you is distinguished, and you're particularly distinguished to be affiliated with a school like this one. It's true, and your principal said it when he told me, "You have 1,300 of these and we've got one." Schools succeed one at a time. And one of the exciting things for me is to see a school like this, a high school of some 500-plus students that does not only succeed, but really exceeds, by setting enormously high standards and creating a community in which the principal values are putting children first and not compromising on the things that you believe are critical to education.

And if we are going to succeed in America today, we are going to do it by replicating those core features that make this school and many others a beacon for what we hope public education would be.

Now the reason I came today is to speak to the students in this school because I believe that I am in a room with real future leaders in America. And every chance I get to speak to future leaders I think is critical. In this room there are going to be leaders in the arts, there are going to be leaders in medicine, you're going to be leaders in medicine and science, leaders in business, leaders in religion, people who will set the gold standard in so many ways in our country. And yet, I wonder whether those people will be leaders in the public life of our nation.

When I was privileged to serve as assistant attorney general, I made the point once a month to go to colleges and high schools to talk informally with students. One of the things that perplexed me and distressed me time and again was how students had turned away from public life. They thought public life is not critical to them. They were concerned about their careers, concerned about the private lives that they were going to live, but somehow did not think public service for the kind of country we have become was critical.

So I'd like to start by saying to each and every one of you that your private lives, your private ambitions and the fields you go into with your family will be deeply, indeed, be profoundly affected by what happened in the public life of our nation. I want you, as you continue your education here and move on to college and on to graduate school, to be ever mindful of the fact that in our constitution we came together to create a more perfect future, and that is the process that each generation must recommit itself to.

Our union is not only not imperfect, but it is far from perfect, and it will never become all of the things that we hope unless each future generation of leaders is prepared to commit itself to do the hard work of justice, the hard work of society, the hard work of articulating a shared value and a shared sense of community that makes this one nation under God, indivisible. That is the challenge, and leadership must rise to the challenge.

We have a remarkable constitutional democracy. When you look today to see what's going on in the Middle East and around the world, we need to realize you have inherited an enormously, extraordinarily valuable thing, this constitutional democracy of ours. And every four years, like we will do next Tuesday, we will hold an election, and every four years power transfers in an orderly fashion. Just think, unsettling though it was, the last election we had ended up in the courts, but it did not up in violence. And while people may have been unhappy, people accepted the results.

That is not the model that is ubiquitously available throughout our world. And whether it remains the model will depend on the commitment of future leaders.

And here we are in the world's greatest democracy and about one in two of our people will actually take the time to vote next week. How sad for us.

And yes, even considering all of these wonderful things, our mission of liberty and equality remains incomplete. Ours is a country with a history built in part upon slavery and a century of Jim Crow and segregation, a destiny for black Americans that remains very incomplete. And that, too, has to be part of the agenda for each new generation of leadership.

And today I believe we stand on the cusp as we move into the early years of this new century of a set of issues that will truly determine what kind of nation we will become.

9/11 changed the face of the world. There is no question that these young people in this room will grow up in an environment in which personal security and national safety will be a dominant concern. And we must remain strong and vigilant to deal with that.

I think the No. 1 issue in our world today is global security. But a close second is the one I'd like to spend some time with you on today, and that is: What kind of nation will we be internally? And to answer that, there is no more important question than whether we will become serious about educating our children in America.

Even though we have a national election, and even though people talk occasionally about education,

I don't think we are remotely cognizant of the fact that we are facing a crisis in America today. If you compare it to Eastern and Western European countries, we have our issues.

If you look at the emerging economies in Asia, our country is going to face increasing competitive pressure. Globalization is going to shrink this world in a way that most of us who are adults in this room would not be able to match. And both the civic strength of our democracy and the power of our economy will be directly related to the quality of the education we provide. We as a society will need to get much more serious about that than we have been.

Let me tell you a little bit about New York City, because I think New York City truly is the prototype of what I'm talking about. There are two themes of which we must remain cognizant: one is excellence, the other is equity. And we need to do both, and do both at a much higher level.

When it comes to excellence, New York City is in many ways a leader. Last week, in both medicine and business, more people from the city were awarded the Nobel Prize than any other place, two of each. Three out of four went to public high school in New York City.

I have a high school, Stuyvesant High School, which is about four or five times the size of this school. Each year Stuyvesant High School has more semifinalists in the Intel National Science Competition than any other high school in the United States.

So, at one end of the spectrum we do foster and support excellence. We need to do more. We need to create more schools that emphasize technology and science. We need to create more schools supporting future engineers and future researchers. But when it comes to excellence, New York City, unlike many urban school districts, has a history and a series of current experiences of which we can justify and be proud.

On the other hand, I think equity needs a lot of work, and here I'm talking about every city in the United States. Ours is the biggest, but it's absolutely prototypical. I need you to get your head around some numbers. I didn't come here to drown you in statistics, but I need you to think about the implications of these facts.

In my school system from grades K through 12, I have 1.1 million students. That's bigger than most cities in the United States. There are 135,000 employees, some 80,000 of whom are teachers, one of the largest work forces in the organization. I have 1,350 schools, and since I keep creating new ones that number will continue to rise. The system has a $15 billion budget, and enormous diversity. New York is the melting pot, our schools reflect that diversity. Thirty-eight percent of our students are Latinos, 34 percent African-American, another 28 percent roughly half-and-half Asian and Caucasian. So it's a predominantly minority school district by any view in the world.

We have students from over 200 different countries attending school in New York, and many are recent arrivals. At any given time somewhere between 12-14 percent of our students are classified as 'English language learners.' They are recent immigrants to America who have come from all over the world and will come out speaking our language.

Close to 60 percent of over 1.1 million students are classified as living in poverty by federal guidelines. Out of that group, approximately 100,000 leave the school system every year. By and large we are failing those students, and failing them significantly.

In New York, like in Ohio, we have a thing called a Regents diploma, which is what you need to graduate from high school to be prepared for college. It's reasonably rigorous; it's a benchmark that's worth taking note of. One in five children in New York City public schools- one in five- gets a Regents diploma. Only 1 in 10 African-American and Latino students receive a Regents diploma.

In order to compensate for that we've created a 'watered-down' diploma. The state threatens to outlaw it, but we call it a local diploma, and we essentially lower the standards on our Regents exams. Overall, another 3 in 10 students get a local diploma. That means about half of our students come out of our high schools with a diploma.

And if you think that about 90,000 to 100,000 students will leave each year, that means somewhere between 45,000 and 50,000 students a year, half of my children, come out of school with nothing. Not prepared for civic society, not prepared for the economy they will face.

Now, how long can we continue with a system that is basically batting .500 when it comes to the future of our country?

And let me be clear with you: New York is not an outlier. I think most people who study this subject will tell you that New York City is probably one of the highest-performing major cities in terms of education.

These problems are neither unique nor are they being exaggerated by focusing on my particular city. What I submit to you is that if we continue down that path, it will say volumes about the kind of country we will be. Globalization, the threats to our society, the world we live in, are not going to tolerate an increasing number of students at that percentage who are totally unprepared.

Indeed, at a time when we are failing students, the global demands are getting higher on those very students, not lower. that is why I am thrilled to have been chosen by the mayor of New York City, Michael Bloomberg, to be what we call the Chancellor of New York City schools.

But if you think about it, why me? Why do you choose somebody who is not a career educator, who has not had a career inside the system? I think that reflects part of the transformation that we are now seeing. It's a transformation in which people are getting serious about the fact that incremental or minor tinkering or, worse yet, cheerleading, is not going to change education for America.

In our largest cities today, New York, Los Angeles, Chicago, Philadelphia, San Diego and others, they have what they call a "nontraditional superintendent," which is another fancy way of saying someone who knows nothing about the field but they've put in charge. These are people who come in with an entirely different perspective, but they are people who I think are appointed when they're appointed because they are change agents, not incrementalists.

If you study history, you can look at the 1960s and see the transformation of American business. Look at the '80s and you'll see the transformation of the American military. I believe that we are now going through the beginning of a process of transformation of American education. It won't be easy, and it won't happen overnight.

What I also find astonishing is people who ask after a year or two years, "Well, why haven't you solved these problems?" These problems are highly resistant to change, and the level of change we need will require transforming the culture of education.

To me there are a couple of core ingredients. The first is your value system. When I got a chance to talk to your principal before, he said to me, and I can tell it came from the heart, "At our school children come first." We called our reform initiative in New York "Children First," precisely because I think in too many educational situations the interests of adults are placed ahead of the interests of the children.

If we don't reorient those values, we're not going to succeed. Teaching is not a challenge. Teaching is a call. Teachers should be properly paid and properly supported, but teaching is a calling and at its core its value has to be "children first."

The second thing we need to do, and on this point there is still a lot of controversy, is to not only insist on standards, but insist on rigorous testing to enforce standards. For so long we have fooled ourselves into thinking that we are going to promote children through the system to the end game, and that somehow it would take care of itself.

Only now, when we insist upon rigorous measures can we actually see that which we have long known but have been afraid to articulate. That is, most of our children are failing, and failing miserably. We don't have a lot of kids in New York who can read but aren't passing the reading tests. We have far more trouble. We have many students who cannot read.

To that end, our mayor decided he was going to put an end to this insidious practice of socially promoting children. That is, moving them ahead in their class regardless of whether they advanced the material. As a result of that practice, the outcomes I gave you before are the outcomes that dominate our school system. People don't believe this, but I can take you into hundreds of high schools in New York City and I will show you children who are not reading. Many of whom can't decode, much less comprehend, what's in a simple book.

We promoted these children, some of them in high school, year after year because it served the needs of the system that was unwilling to be accountable for its children.

We decided to put an end to that in third grade. And this caused an enormous controversy in our city. But who were we fooling? What good can it do for a child to pass him or her through the system to the point where he or she at 15, 16, 17 or 18 years old cannot read?

Miracles are wonderful, especially in a school like this, and I'll continue to pray for them. But we also have a rational decision making process. Turning around tens of thousands of kids when they're in 9th, 10th, 11th grade is a daunting challenge no matter where you are. We can do a lot better.

The second important thing we need to focus on is one of the things I talked to you about here today: leadership. Being a principal of a school is an absolutely critical function, and we need both to invest in leadership, to support leadership, but also to select leadership based purely on merit. And when people don't perform as school leaders, we need to find another job for them.

This is a not a tenured position, and should not be a tenured position, and so much depends on it.

And yet in most school systems in the United States, principals are tenured and its very hard to remove them.

In New York City we've done several things. I've been fortunate to raise almost $60 million to create a rigorous leadership training program. Working with captains of industry and educators, we have put together a training program whereby each year we start with 90 aspiring principals and put them through a rigorous 15-month training period. And at the end of that 15 months, we then deploy them in our schools.

One of the things we learn quickly is that out of 90, we consider it fortunate if 75 make it, because our demands are high. Not everyone who shows up gets to be a principal.

In addition, last year for the first time I removed close to 50 principals for non-performance. Again, it was something that caused a great deal of controversy in our city. But if we don't get leadership right the rest will not follow.

It is obvious to me when you meet a principal like your principal that you have great leadership. And I bet it's obvious to the teachers in this building, and it's obvious to the students in this building. In the absence of that it will not happen. And if the principal shift becomes the last stop on the way to a pension, as it often is in the public school system, we make a catastrophic mistake.

The third thing you need to do is you need to

have a different view of the teaching profession. There's a report that came out recently by a group called the Teaching Commission. There's a line there that I found haunting, which is our teachers want excellence but the public school system rarely supports excellence or rewards excellence. A system that does not reward excellence is unlikely to inspire.

We need to be able to have the flexibility to create pay differentials to reward people for performance and to make sure that the best and brightest don't flee *from* our profession, but flee *to* our profession.

What I have called for in New York is a different kind of labor management, one that recognizes teachers as the professionals that they are, but also recognizes that by rewarding excellence we will inspire excellence in our school system.

Finally, all of this must be tied together with a system of true accountability. Inputs are not what we need to measure an education, and yet that is what all the public discourse is about. Money, as important as it is, is not nearly as important as how you spend the money you have. And where you put your investments will be critical to student outcomes. And the lesson, too, is that until we think of our strategies in terms of outcomes, and in terms of accountability and values, we're not going to change public education.

I'm enormously proud to work for Michael Bloomberg. Why is that? When Michael Bloomberg became mayor of New York City, the first thing he did was go to Albany and say, "I want to restructure the legislation so that I, the mayor, am accountable to the city for public education."

Now let's be honest with each other. He knows he's got to run four short years, or by the time legislation is passed, three and a half years later. No city in America today has turned around urban education. Yet Michael Bloomberg said, "When I run for re-election I will stand before the city and say I am accountable for public education."

By standing up and sending a signal to change the system, what he is saying is that until all of us are accountable to the children in our school system, we will not create the kind of culture of success that is absolutely necessary to transform education.

Let me leave you with the following thought: Many people have said to me that you can't do this, that children who grow up in poverty, children who come from broken homes, and children whose parents are not readers will not succeed in education today. Indeed, there are some who argue that until we fix poverty we won't be able to fix education.

I think that it's one of the most corrosive thoughts on the public stage today. I know because I have seen it time and again that even the most difficult, most challenged students can succeed when confronted with high standards in a school that will support those children and will respect those children, but will demand much of those children. The school in which the motto is "children first" will be one in which children will succeed time and again.

Children and many people will try to explain away as being from that family or that background or that circumstance and therefore not likely to be educated. We can do this. And, indeed, if America wants to deal with an issue such as poverty, I assure you we will never fix poverty unless until we fix education. It is an entirely doable challenge. Not easy, and it will not be accomplished overnight, but it's entirely doable.

So today I come here to St. Charles and I say to each one of you young men that when you think about the world view, think about your responsibilities to that world. And if there is an area where you can make a tremendous difference, it is in transformation of the education of our society, with nothing more important to the future of the world people live in.

Thank you for the opportunity to be with you today.

- October 27, 2004

In January 2011, **JOEL I. KLEIN** *became CEO of the Education Division (now called Amplify) and Executive Vice President, Office of the Chairman, at News Corporation, where he also serves on the Board of Directors.*

Prior to that, Mr. Klein was Chancellor of the New York City Department of Education, where he oversaw a system of over 1,600 schools with 1.1 million students, 136,000 employees and a $22 billion budget. He launched Children First in 2002, a comprehensive reform strategy that has brought coherence and capacity to the system and resulted in significant increases in student performance.

He is a former Chairman and CEO of Bertelsmann, Inc., a media company, and served as Assistant U.S. Attorney General in charge of the Antitrust Division of the U.S. Department of Justice until September 2000, and was Deputy White House Counsel to President Clinton from 1993-1995. Mr. Klein entered the Clinton administration after 20 years of public and private legal work in Washington, D.C.

Mr. Klein received his Bachelor of Arts from Columbia University where he graduated magna cum laude in 1967, and earned his J.D. from Harvard Law School in 1971, also graduating magna cum laude. He has received honorary degrees from Amherst College, Columbia University, Dartmouth College, Duke University, Fordham Law School, Georgetown Law Center, Macaulay Honors College at CUNY, Manhattanville College, New York Law School and St. John's School of Education. He was selected by Time Magazine as one of Ten People who Mattered in 1999, by U.S. News and World Report as One of America's 20 Best Leaders in 2006, and was given the prestigious NYU Lewis Rudin Award in 2009 and Manhattan Institute Alexander Hamilton Award in 2011.

4

F. Russell Hittinger, Ph.D.

on
Civility in American Law

"We are very fortunate because we got the relationship between religion and the state right from the very beginning."

Of course, the topic that was assigned to me was civility in American law. My remarks this afternoon are taken from the fact that we have a Supreme Court bitterly divided. Case after case, for 35 years, five-to-four decisions. They're bitterly divided over the constitutional place of religion in our public life. And we are now at a somewhat historic moment of having two new Supreme Court justices and, I think, a third within a year or two. So that is the context for my thoughts.

During the 1988 presidential campaign, George Bush senior, that's George Herbert Walker Bush, reflected on his adventures during the second World War when he was shot down over a Japanese-held island, Chichi-Jima. And, then-Vice President Bush, on the campaign trail, said, and I quote here, "Was I scared floating in a little yellow raft off the coast of an enemy-held island, setting a world record for paddling? Of course I was. But what does this say to you in times like that? Well, you go back to fundamental values. Well, I thought about Mother, Dad, the strength I got from them. And God, and faith and separation of church and state."

You've got to love a country in which a future president of the United States, summoning one last thought before his imminent demise, would contemplate so cerebrally the relationship between church and state. In fact, when I first heard this back in 1988, it seemed so daffy, so confused, that I thought he must have hit his head when he parachuted out of the plane. But over the years, I've come to think this was quite an honest and accurate reflection.

We are very fortunate because we got the relationship between religion and the state right from the very beginning. We are one of the only nations and, I believe, in the West, the only nation that never had a religious civil war. France, Spain, England, Germany, Ireland, all experienced religious civil wars, sometimes more than once. Even Canada, our very civil neighbors to the North, were divided between French Catholic and English-speaking Anglicans, armed to the teeth.

Mexico to our south experienced illegal persecution of religion in the early 20th century that exceeded what was done in communist countries. So is what's going on in Iraq today, where there is no consensus at all of what belongs to religion and what belongs to the state.

So allow me to propose that the primary importance of civility is harmony between religious and state authorities. By harmony, I mean not only that religion and state should respect each other's proper spirit, but also that neither religion nor government should ever attempt to divide a culture. Civic and religious loyalties are enmeshed in culture. And cultures, unlike pieces of property, cannot be split into two or more parts.

We have two powers, each with its own proper sphere, but it's impossible to have two societies or cultures.

In our country this mark of civility is important because, by every quantitative estimation, we are the most religious country in the developed world, with the possible exception of Poland.

In the middle of the 19th century, French sociologist Alexis de Tocqueville noted after his trip to America, "The morality and intelligence of a democratic people would risk no fewer dangers than its business and its industry if the government came to take the place of associations everywhere. Sentiments and ideas renew themselves, the heart is enlarged, and the human mind is developed only by the reciprocal action of men upon one another... For the Americans, the idea of Christianity and liberty are so completely minimal, that it is almost impossible to get them to conceive of one without the other."

And many decades later, another Catholic visitor to our country, the Catholic essayist G.K. Chesterton, noted that America is a nation that is the soul of the church. Both Tocqueville and Chesterton noted that there's no need for a rivalry between church and state in America for the simple reason that rivalry doesn't exist in the everyday lives of Americans.

And it's still true. If anything, Americans are more religious today than they were a century ago, according to a 2004 national study on religion and politics. Only 3.2 percent of Americans have absolutely no religious convictions or practices. Basically, 3.2 percent of Americans are practically atheists. But according to a recent Gallup poll, only 3 percent of Americans believe they are not loved by God. Now, do the math between those two polls. You've got to be amazed at a country in which more people believe they are loved by God than believe that God exists.

It reminds me of a famous city in Poland where I teach every summer. During communist times people would say, "Polish communists do not believe in God, but they absolutely believe that Mary is his mother."

Moreover, a 2004 national survey shows that religion does not translate into hard political polarization. Despite what we hear on television, and what the media reports (red state, blue state), religious believers are about 40 percent Republican, 40 percent Democrat, 20 percent whatever.

Americans are also basically a tolerant society. Last summer, Newsweek reported (and even I was sort of struck by this) 80 percent of religious believers in the United States, including 68 percent of evangelicals, are convinced that more than one faith would be a path to salvation. This is the kind of thing that gives the preachers, rabbis and priests indigestion when they hear about it.

About 20 percent of Americans change their religion at least once during adulthood. Still, other polls show that while 75 percent of Americans support posting the Ten Commandments in public places, 85 percent do not believe that government officials should turn their own religious convictions into law.

Now, that looks like a contradiction, but it isn't. Americans do not want the government stripping religion into the public culture. By the same token, they don't want religion to be enforced by law.

Far from being a contradiction, I believe this a mark of American civility. Civil and religious authorities ought to accommodate each other for the sake of the common good. Now, for its part, religion has a vast civilizing role in our culture.

Permit me just briefly to speak of my own family. My grandmother was the child of Scottish lumberjack the wilds of Montana in the late nineteenth century. Her parents had no good means of support. They left her on the doorstep of a convent of nuns, where she was baptized and raised during her early years.

My father, after World War II, used the G.I. Bill

to go to Villanova University, where he joined ROTC and became a Marine Corps Officer. My brother and I both went to Notre Dame on Social Security benefits from our deceased father.

In my career, I've taught at Fordham, Princeton, Catholic University of America, all private, religiously founded schools. My current position is at a Presbyterian university, where I hold an endowed chair by a Catholic oil family, and where I teach Baptists and Pentecostals.

My healthcare plan is at a Catholic hospital. My son went to a diocesan high school. Now he attends a private university originally endowed by Baptists.

That's my story. But it's not just my story, it's the story of millions of Americans. What would our lives look like without the civilizing role of religion?

Of the 900 religiously affiliated colleges and universities in the United States, 220 are Catholic. Get this: that's more than 20 times the number of independent religious colleges in all Europe. At the primary and secondary school levels, Catholic schools enroll almost 2.5 million students, 20 percent of whom are minorities. According to *The NonProfit Times*, those who regularly practice religion give more than two-thirds of all the charitable dollars in the United States, and in fact they give double than that of non-religious people. Interestingly, religious practitioners donate more to secular organizations than those who call themselves secularists.

Some 622 hospitals in the United States are

Catholic. You can take the example of your own patron saint. During the plague and famine in 1576 in Milan, Charles Borromeo tried to feed 60,000 or 70,000 people daily. He borrowed money that required years to repay.

When all the civil authorities left to avoid the plague, he stayed in the city where he ministered to the sick and the dying.

This kind of dedication to the common good is seen every day in this country, in AIDS clinics, in hospices, homes for single mothers, and most recently on the Gulf Coast, in which religious orders were the first ones into the disaster area.

So here, it is appropriate for me to pause, and give this word to the students. When you leave St. Charles Prep, there's nothing more important you should do than supporting this institution and other institutions like it. Do it out of gratitude, for what you can see, do it for the sake of your own kids. But at the end of the day, you're doing it for the sake of society. Because in these kinds of institutions, minds are enlightened, careers are formed, broken bodies are mended, souls are inspired. Don't forget to do that.

Now, everything I've said should strike you as common sense. But why do we hear of such a constant struggle in our nation courts between religion and government?

A case in point: On October 29, 1997, federal judge Ira DeMent issued a permanent injunction prohibiting religious activities in or around public schools in Alabama. Forbidden activities include Bible and religious devotions, scriptural readings, distribution of religious materials, texts, announcements, and discussions of a devotional or religious nature regardless of whether those discussions were initiated, led by, or engaged in by students.

Judge DeMent expressly enjoined schools not to pray in times of emergency or national crisis. He also threatened to hold in contempt of court student athletes who pray for another student who is seriously injured during practice or on the football field.

The most notable and ominous part of DeMent's injunction was his order to set up a system of monitors to enter classrooms, visit sporting events, observe any and all activities in public schools in order to collect points and to verify compliance towards the injunction. A network of civilian police to patrol schools and report any expression of religion- in Alabama! Even the parent-teacher organization must be enlisted to gather information for the federal court. Public schools also are required to conduct mandatory in-service training for faculty and administrators. Teachers and administrators had to be subjected to re-education, there's no other word for it, and forced to learn the opinions of the Federal courts on the nature of the First Amendment.

For the next four years, the injunction would occupy the attention of the 11th Circuit Court of Appeals, which eventually, to everyone's relief, pulled most of the teeth out of the injunction.

But Judge DeMent's injunction is a token of the dissatisfying plight of the federal judiciary on matters religious. How did the judicial branch become so completely swamped in religious litigation? And swamped is an apt metaphor. Judge DeMent's injunction was tied to a case called Chandler v. James that began in 1993. That case was tied in turn to a 1985 case called Wallace v. Jaffree. All told, 16 years of litigation and just this one.

How did it happen that members of the Supreme Court that routinely refer to each other's First Amendment opinions as, and here I quote, "totally incorrect," "unsound," "bordering on anarchy," "inherently ethnocentric," "outright perverse,", "ridiculous," "pure fantasy," "pernicious," "absurd," "bordering on paranoia," and as "an Orwellian rewriting of history." And those are not all taken from Justice Scalia.

No other area of the Court's jurisprudence, including abortion, invokes such a personal and ideological bitterness.

Now, we all know the words of the First Amendment: "Congress shall make no law respecting the establishment of religion, or prohibiting the free exercise thereof." This constitutional law has never been breached. Congress has never established a church or a religion. And to this day, the Supreme Court has never found an act of Congress to be in violation of this Establishment Clause. Why, then, all the argument?

A very famous American jurist, Oliver Wendell Holmes, once said, "A page of history is worth more than a volume of logic." Here's a page from his book. First fact: From the time of the early Republic until the 1940s, the religion clauses in the First Amendment were an extraordinarily serene section of constitutional law. From the adoption of the Bill of Rights in 1791, until Everson v. Board of Education in 1947, there's not a single Establishment Clause case involving state or municipal ordinance. That's 156 years.

Of all the different kinds of crises faced by the American people, slavery, wars, and so on, governmental establishment of religion was not one of them. I know of no significant public person, newspaper or political party, from the time of the early republic to the 1940s, that claims the establishment of religion is a problem in American political institutions, either at the federal or the state level.

Massachusetts had abandoned what remained of its established church in 1833. And no state has an established church since that time. But, fact number two: Beginning in the late 1940s and continuing into our time, the federal courts have detected literally thousands of instances of establishing religions in the southern states.

Here are the options: either there has been an epidemic of constitutional crime or virtually every state and municipality in the nation accelerated dramatically in the 1940s to our time. Or, the federal courts have just profoundly misestimated of the scope of the First Amendment.

The first explanation is implausible. No one can believe that in the 1940s Americans suddenly, and without precedent, found themselves in an epidemic of religious establishment.

This was my parents' generation. They came back from World War II, they were moving to the suburbs, they were worried about having two cars. To think that that 1940s generation was trying to establish a religion is ludicrous.

In fact, I know of no instance in which a state or municipal government since 1833 has ever admitted on the record that it had tried to establish a religion or was doing anything that could be contended to establish a religion.

In other words, we haven't had any establishment of religion by the government since 1833. So, how can the Court be picking out thousands of instances of it?

I think the problem is a self-inflicted wound on the part of the Court itself.

In 1947, the Supreme Court ruled that henceforth, the Establishment Clause would be applied to the states and municipal governments, but that establishment means not only trying to set up a state church or religion, but it also means any governmental preference for a religion over another religion. And the next year, in 1948, the court went on to rule that states must create religion-free zones in public schools. By implication, all of the other public institutions and places would have to follow the game guidelines. That is, they have to create religion-free zones. In other words, the Court, however well intentioned, got itself into the business of attempting to separate religion from ordinary culture.

And the floodgates of litigation opened, like a yard sale in Oklahoma, almost everything in American public life looks suspiciously religious: pledges of allegiance, coins, timed release programs, inside the school, off school grounds, taxis, calendars, textbooks, maps, bible readings, prayer in school, prayer in Congress, prayer in the executive branch, national days of prayer, non-negotiable historic uses of the bible, Sunday closing laws, the national anthem, chaplains, chaplains in the legislature, chaplains in the armed forces, chaplains in the prisons. And the court had not even tackled that.

Football games, moments of silence, Christmas nativity scenes, menorahs, yarmulkes, Native American burial grounds, Amish education, evolution, city seals, science textbooks, sign language interpretation, the mystical aspect of social security numbers, posting commandments, the Declaration of Independence, and the Ohio motto, "With God all things are possible."

So, by 1971, the majority of the Supreme Court realized that they had made a mess of things. And the wall of separation metaphor, was, as Chief Justice Burger admitted, a "blurred, indistinct, invariable barrier." He went on to say that total separation is not possible in an absolute sense. And so, instead of a wall, he proposed a three-fold test called the "Lemon Test": Government action must have a secular purpose, the primary effect of the government action neither inhibit nor advance religion, and the government must not become entangled with religion.

All this seemed reasonable enough in 1971, except for the fact in case after case the court split 5-4 in every case, or in almost every case, that the test was applied. Among other things, it seemed entirely subjective whether or not a government law had a religious motivation, or whether a law or policy advanced or inhibited a religion.

In order to save the Supreme Court's religion jurisprudence from becoming completely secular, Justice Sandra Day O'Connor, recently appointed to the Supreme Court, nominated by President Reagan, proposed yet another test: In order to detect whether a state or local government is establishing a religion, we should adopt the standpoint of a reasonable observer, mindful of history, purpose, context, an observer of indeterminable religious affiliation who knows all the facts and circumstances surrounding the allegedly religious display or event. Thus the purposes of the government are to be judged not according to the government's own actions and statements, but by a private third party who is entirely fictional, someone who has the kind of perspective possessed only by a political activist and his lawyers. And sure enough, rather than focusing or combing the litigation on religion, the floodgates were opened even more.

In a number of cases, the court ruled that presidential or congressional prayers are OK because these prayers, the court reasoned, can be ignored, or they have lost their religious significance, despite being prayers by clergy to an almighty God.

The court also ruled that financial aid to parochial colleges is OK, but not to high schools, reasoning that students under the age of 18 hear or have to hear a message of endorsement of religion when the government gives money to their high schools, whereas students over 18 don't care one way or the other.

Writing for the majority, in one of the famous Nativity scene cases, Lynch v. Donnelly in 1984, Chief Justice Berger commented that the Nativity scene depicting a reverence to the Wise Men or the Christ Child simply sends a message of seasonal good cheer rather than religion. In fact, he went on to say that it just stirs people up to shop more.

Why is it religious? Justice Berger said, "Because there are these candy canes and reindeers with Santa Claus around the Nativity scene that camouflaged the religious message." No one thought to inform Chief Justice Berger, candy canes are a Christian symbol of the body and blood of Christ, or that the deer represents the stag panting for salvation in Psalm 42. Much less, an even simpler point, is that Santa Claus is a Christian saint.

One year later, in Wallace v. Jaffree, which began

the problems in Alabama, one minute of silence in an Alabama school is ruled to be the establishment of religion because the legislature had a religious motivation for the silence. So, a display having undeniable religious content, the Christ child being adored, was not religion, while the event having no external religious content was deemed and establishment of religion.

Four years later, in a case called Allegheny County, the court struck down a display of the Nativity scene surrounded by poinsettias. Yet it upheld the Menorah, also set up on public property in Pittsburgh, because it was dwarfed by a 45-foot Christmas tree, minimizing the likelihood that the Menorah would be taken as a governmental endorsement of religion. Again, no one bothered to note that an evergreen tree is a traditional symbol of eternal life.

And this brings us to two Ten Commandments decisions of last June and July, two decisions the Supreme Court handed down. Displays of the Ten Commandments in Texas were upheld, while displays in Kentucky were struck down. All told, the members of the Court filed nine different opinions. There are only nine members of the Court.

In the case in Texas, the Court had to consider some 17 monuments and 21 historical markers on 22 acres surrounding the Texas state capitol. These included Heroes of the Alamo, volunteer firefighters, Terry's Texas Rangers, Texas cowboys, The Spanish-American War, Texas National Guard, the Ten

Commandments and Tribute to Texas School Children.

Now, the Ten Commandments display was donated in 1961 by the Fraternal Order of Eagles of Texas, along with famous film director, Cecil B. Demille, who was, at that time, filming "The Ten Commandments," the movie, who gave the money for the displays as promotion for his film. The historical record showed that the Eagles' purpose was nonsectarian, but clearly religious. They believed that disseminating the divinely sanctioned world message of the Ten Commandments would help persuade young men and women to observe civilized standards of behavior.

Now, in this particular case, the court managed to produce six discrete opinions. And at the end of the day, the decisions seemed to turn on one simple fact: The display sat for 40 years before anyone bothered to sue the government. Therefore, an objective observer would not detect a religious message.

In Kentucky, on the other hand, two counties had displayed the Commandments in their courthouses. And they were, indeed, an establishment of religion. Again, the decision seemed determined on the simple fact. The counties were sued and during the litigation, they twice revised the displays to make them less controversial. No virtue goes unpunished.

Writing for the majority, Justice Souter reasoned that the purpose of these Kentucky counties was motivated by religion from the very onset, because they kept revising those displays. He wrote, "If someone in the government hides religious motive so well that the objective observer, acquainted with the text, legislative history, and implementation of the statute, cannot see it, then without something more the government does not make a divisive announcement that in itself amounts to taking religious sides. *A secret motive stirs up no strife and does nothing to make outsiders of nonadherents…*"

In other words, the misperception of a hypothetical objective observer was decisive. If the observer cannot detect the fraudulent purpose, the government action stands. If the observer mistakenly detects a fraudulent motive, then the government action has to be struck down. That's simply not an exercise of constitutional law. I don't know what it is.

Now, the Court has had 55 years to put into order the house of its Establishment Clause jurisprudence, and its plainly a failure. Eighty percent of Americans still love these displays. The number of Americans who want prayer in school keeps going up because of these controversies.

And according to opinion polls, even those who call themselves true separationalists cannot muster a majority against religious symbols in public places. Interestingly enough, there is one public display of religion that 52 percent of Americans don't like, and that's prayer before high school football games. Isn't it interesting? It's not displays of the Ten Commandments, its prayer before high school football games.

Now, there are more than 4,000 of these religious displays in public places, parks and courthouses nationwide. Is the federal judiciary really going to make the Constitution tip and turn for all of these controversies? The answer is no.

Now, after last summer's decisions, looking back to this, both sides started gearing up for more litigation. There are really more people who love this kind of controversy. One group, the Christian Defense Coalition, announced plans to place displays similar to the ones in Texas in 100 additional towns and cities. Another group, the Freedom From Religion Foundation, announced plans to erect a monument for free thinkers and atheists in the Texas capitol buildings. This jurisprudence of the Court satisfies no one but the radicals on both sides.

Now, I don't believe we can ever return to those sentiments quite so simple and naïve as George Bush's thoughts about Mom and Dad and God and faith and separation of church and state. But, when I make my Christmas wish list this year for Santa Claus, I will wish for the Court to get itself out of symbolic politics and involving religion, get itself out. It makes a monkey out of the Court. It creates an atmosphere of persecution. It trivializes the Establishment Clause. Just stop and think about this.

Funds have been appropriated for the victims in the Gulf Coast. It has been proposed that they reimburse religious believers and organizations. On my count, it will be the single largest transfer of your tax dollars to religion in the history of the United States. Now, that's something worth having an argument about. Menorahs and Christmas trees, please, give us a break. The Establishment Clause is more important than that.

But at the end of the day, it creates a totally unnecessary conflict between the two great civilizing forces of our culture, religion and government. On my count, only two sitting members of the Supreme Court are satisfied with the Establishment Clause jurisprudence used by the Court in the past 35 years. And I suspect the Supreme Court is now one vote away from getting out of this symbolic religion and politics business. If her nomination is confirmed by the Senate, Harriet Myers will be that vote one way or the other. Stay tuned.

Thank you for giving me the opportunity.

- October 7, 2005

Since 1996, **DR. F. RUSSELL HITTINGER** *has been the incumbent of the William K. Warren Chair of Catholic Studies at the University of Tulsa, where he is also a Research Professor in the School of Law. Professor Hittinger specializes in issues of philosophy, theology and law.*

From 2002-2005 he was the Chair of the Department of Philosophy and Religion. He currently supervises the Certificate in Political Philosophy.

He has taught at Fordham University and at the Catholic University of America, and has taught as a Visiting Professor at Princeton University, New York University, Charles University in Prague, and at the Pontifical Università Regina Apostolorum in Rome. In 2000, he was a Senior Research Fellow at the Notre Dame Center for Ethics and Culture, where he is on the board of Advisors. Since 2001, he has been a member of the Pontificia Academia Sancti Thomae Aquinatis (Pontifical Academy of St. Thomas Aquinas), to which he was elected a full member (ordinarius) in 2004, and two years later was elected to the consilium or governing board (as consigliere).

On Sept. 8, 2009, Pope Benedict XVI appointed Professor Hittinger an ordinarius in the Pontifical Academy of Social Sciences. He is one of two academics in the world to serve on two Pontifical academies.

His 85 books and articles have appeared on the University of Notre Dame Press, Oxford University Press, Columbia University Press, Fordham University Press, the Review of Metaphysics, the Review of Politics, and several law journals (American and European).

His article "Privacy and Liberal Legal Culture" was part of a collection of articles that won the Silver Gavel Award of the American Bar Association in 1991. In May 1997, the John Templeton Foundation placed him on the Templeton Honor Roll for Teaching in the Liberal Arts. He has twice received the Josephine Yalch Zekan Award for the Best Scholarly Article in Faith and Law.

5

Archbishop Celestino Migliore

on

Integrity, Truth and Fraternity

"It is not for nothing that Merriam Webster reports that in our day integrity and truthiness are the most searched words."

I was really happy to accept Mr. Dilenschneider's invitation to visit St. Charles Preparatory School and meet you today in the context of the Borromean lecture. I find it interesting that Mr. Dilenschneider wanted to call this series of conversations with you "Borromean Lectures."

Charles Borromeo belonged to an aristocratic family, who in the European tradition had its own coat of arms. The family crest had a trio of rings intertwined in such a way that removing any of the rings would cause the entire structure to fall apart. And today even physicists use the term "Borromean" to describe atomic nuclei that behave in a similar way, so that if any one constituent is removed the last of the nucleus disintegrates.

Well, I did not discuss this beforehand with Mr. Dilenschneider, but knowing his dedication to solid information for young students and excellent education, I venture to say he intended these lectures to focus on those basic values that are intertwined in such a way that the lack of or lessening of any of them would cause the entire society to fall apart.

And he gave me a *tabula rasa* for the topic of this conversation. However, the theme for my talk today came to me from one of his annual reports. I'm sure many of you know that Dilenschneider Group, based in New York and Chicago, publishes biannual trend forecasting reports and a number of special reports which focus on critical thinking and how we might apply that in our life, our business, or whatever other pursuit we follow. And within the set of noteworthy trends for 2007, the 34th report identified the two most searched words on the website of the authoritative Merriam Webster dictionary. In 2005 it was "integrity." And in 2006 it was "truthiness."

Well, truthiness is a neologism coined by a comedian on a satirical TV program and refers to the quality of preferring concepts or facts one wishes to be true rather than concepts or facts known to be true. Nevertheless, it points out that our society has a problem with the concept of truth. And yet truth and integrity, once they're left out by individuals in society, they become virtuous and can well be considered two indispensable rings that build, sustain, and season with happiness our contemporary society. I also like to mention happiness when it comes to the list of ingredients for a sane, endurable society.

Three years ago we celebrated the 55th anniversary of the Universal Declaration of Human Rights at the United Nations in New York. And I deliberately spoke of happiness as the ultimate scope of human rights. And walking out of the General Assembly hall the representative of a neighboring country remarked, "You mention happiness, yet there is no mention of happiness in the UN declaration. You may have confused it with the American declaration of the rights and duties of man." "You're right," I replied. "It's too bad that the UN declaration misses this point and that we have to borrow it, although unapologetically."

According to the American Declaration of Independence, the principal aim of human rights is to permit us to obtain happiness. Without happiness as its ultimate goal and parameter, the human right's philosophy and practice can easily drift towards mere litigiousness and simply playing favor of those who can't afford enough resources and power to read over their case.

But now let us turn our attention for a moment to integrity and truthiness. The etymology of integrity comes from the Latin objective *integer*. I know that President Cavello is a professor in Latin, so he must have told you that *integer* means whole, complete. Integrity comprises the personal inner sense of wholeness deriving from honesty and consistent uprightness of character. It is often understood not only as a consistent and coherent behavior, but as a mindset, a lifestyle, and a discovery of some truth.

Allow me to give an example from my own personal experience. Mr. Cavello introduced me as the representative of the Pope at the United Nations in New York. And you may think that this is something I chose to do or that I may have had an inclination towards this type of work, but it's nothing of the sort. I come from a family with no experience or tradition of diplomacy. Therefore, I had no idea what this work entailed.

I was born and raised in the northern region of Italy near Turin, where last year we had the Olympic Winter Games. And when I was a boy, though I belonged to no religious family, I had many friends who were altar boys. Everyone spent a lot of time together. And there I knew a priest who I admired very much because he was a wise man and had the ability of using his gifts for the service of others. And this priest knew a lot about many things and was a man who was accessible to his people 24/7. His holistic character, his wisdom, his availability to serve the poorest of the poor fascinated me. And I said to myself that I wanted to be like him. I did not yet know at the time what it meant to be a priest, but I wanted to be like him, like the pastor who put himself at the service of all.

With this in mind I entered the seminary and began my studies and gradually learned what it meant to be a priest. And shortly after my ordination, my bishop called me to his office and informed me that I was being sent to Rome to begin specialized studies for the diplomatic representations of the Holy See around the world.

I thought it was a bad dream. I knew nothing of this kind of work. In fact, it seemed totally contrary to my ideals. I was afraid that it was bureaucratic work, office work, in which I would lose touch with ordinary people. My immediate response was that I was unable to accept. But he insisted, saying, "Look at the gospel, Peter was a fisherman. He never attended a school, he only knew how to fish, and yet he left everything and began to follow Jesus."

In due course, he who always lived in Palestine and spoke only Aramaic, got into a boat and went to Rome, which was the capital of the world at the time. He rowed with many people. He spoke frequently to the first Christian community and had to learn Latin since that was the language of the Romans. For a man who barely knew his own geography of Galilee and the skill of fishing, Jesus made him a man capable of comforting life in the capital of the world.

Matthew, likewise, was a tax collector. He knew how to add and to collect other people's taxes. Nothing more. He decided to follow Jesus and became a writer who we admire to this day 2000 years later whenever we read the Gospel According to Matthew.

So with that I accepted my bishop's invitation, having faith in his words, and I never regretted having said yes. I feel proud, not of myself, but of Him with a capital H, God, who has called me. Of Him who showed me my own wholeness and proposed things far beyond what I was able to think or imagine. Of Him who I once accepted and has followed me, has given me perseverance, tenacity, the willingness to go forward, and the courage to start again after difficulties in order to maintain the integrity of his plan.

Well, what St. Charles Preparatory School does is offer you a diploma of the highest academic standards and offers you the ways and means to obtain the highest level of personal, human, spiritual and social achievement. In your study of physics you most likely came across that famous quote by Archimedes: "Give me a lever long enough and a place to stand and I can move the earth." Well, our world, our society, desperately needs a jolt.

Any successful school such as yours strives to give its students the lever long enough in the form of the highest level of education. In addition, here you are given the most important element, a place to stand to use that lever that is your own wholeness and integrity, your personal, communal and ecclesial relationship with God. It's up to you to make good use of that lever and to treasure the transcendent place to stand, which I hope will be for you a source of personal and social clarity.

Now the second word, truthiness, as I said before, is a satirical term popularized on the "The Colbert Report" in 2005 in reference to those who claim to know something intuitively, instinctively with no regard for evidence and logic, to intellectual examination or actual facts. "We are at the point where what constitutes truth is a question on a lot of people's minds and truth has become up for grabs," said Merriam Webster President John Morse. The yearning to discover the truth is as old as humankind. The question about truth and fact is not limited to leaving it in one's own conscience, but it is meant to be of public relevance. It refers not only to the truth discovered by an individual in a specific situation or historical epic, but also a truth recognized by the community. And this is our problem today.

In the daily political debate, in all countries, often we no longer understand what's right and what's wrong. Though based on the same principles, certain premonitions hold opposing ideas. Some speak of something that they know for a fact while others simply contradict the existence of those facts. To deny a factual truth and impossibility for citizens to verify it sounds an alarm regarding the political and mass media conditions. As we often see debates on television, it is no longer the players who govern the game, but it is the game of personal opinions and preferences gathered through polls that control the players. One no longer perceives the difference between facts and opinions. So we are walking, in a way, on quicksand.

It is not for nothing that Merriam Webster reports that in our day integrity and truthiness are the most searched words. The search seems to be prompted not only by intellectual curiosity but by the need we have to understand what's happening to us, to our society, to our world. And hopefully there is also an inner and a strong desire to find a way out of this quicksand and find a more stable ground upon which to build our personal and social life. How can I collaborate with my peers? How can I trust them if some of us have a vision irreducibly different as to what is good and bad, true and false- that is, if all opinions are equally true and equally false?

Someone may say one only needs to apply the principal "live and let live." But let us take the following hypothesis already defined many times in the last century: I'm a Christian or a Muslim or a Jew and my neighbor has the opinion of being superior, and for general interest wants to exterminate Jews or Muslims or Christians and is working to realize this objective. It is not enough to live and let live. One needs to know where to draw the line.

In the early 90s, the American writer Samuel Huntington challenged the international committee with his provocative "Clash of Civilizations." He was not alone in anticipating and describing the epochal problems stemming from a worldwide culture of confrontation among different cultures and religions. He was particularly thought provocative for the clear- cut projection of a clash of civilizations.

In the meantime, precisely in 1995, the United Nations launched a year of tolerance. Tolerance, however, soon proved to be insufficient as a principle to govern relations among human beings, mostly because we lost the notion and the feel for what is right and what is wrong, what we can tolerate and what we cannot tolerate. In this context tolerance has quickly become a synonym of permissiveness and a critical openness of diversity. It has become a selective tool to approach our daily life. Our criteria for tolerance depends on what the politically correct dictates or our personal convictions and prejudices, whereas ethical norms that are commonly considered objective and binding are considered to be the cause for intolerance.

There are those who repeat what Pythagoras said some 2,500 years ago. Pythagoras was a philosopher, a contemporary of Socrates, and he maintained that all opinions are equally true and equally false. But not all are equally useful, and what we need is to find out when they're most useful. But even here one cannot evade the problem of truth because that which I think is a useful truth is distinguished from an apparent usefulness. For example, even alcohol and drugs can make me forget my troubles for a moment and make me happy, but does it deal with true happiness, one that is durable and does not bring with it more disadvantages than advantages? Analyzing the causes of terrorism, we see that behind it there are not only political and sociological causes, but also deep cultural, religious and ideological motivations that in the end have to do with our relation to truth.

Terrorist thinking can be inspired by two trends of thought: nihilists and fundamentalism. Nihilists are those who despair of humanity, of life, of the future.

In their view everything is to be hated and destroyed. Fundamentalism can inspire and encourage terrorist thinking and activity by imposing on others by violent means what it considers to be the truth. As Pope Benedict XVI wrote recently for this message for the 2006 World Day of Peace, "Nihilism and fundamentalism share an erroneous relationship to truth. The nihilist denies the very existence of truth while the fundamentalist claims to be able to impose it by force. And despite their different origins and cultural backgrounds both show a dangerous contempt for human beings and human life and ultimately for the truth itself."

It is often held today that a common human vision does not exist, that there exist only "values cultures" in which some have their own values and their own truths largely incompatible and non-conformable to other cultures. Two years ago, during the debate at the assembly of the United Nations, my delegation was the only one to present a paper on human cloning. We circulated our paper to all the missions and during the debate another delegation, an ambassador from an Asian country, argued that the paper circulated by the Holy See on the matter used arguments that were religious. Imagine! You can't talk religion at the United Nations.

Well, I challenged my colleague to point to a single religious argument in the paper knowing that there weren't any. I said that the Holy See made its case based on right reason. And the ambassador replied, "What is reason? Isn't that a rather western concept?"

This is the absolute central problem of today's cultural panorama, of dire confrontation, and to confront it correctly it seems indispensable to promote a serious reflection on the concept of truth. Socrates has remained the symbol of the clash between truth and politics, between truth and popular opinion. Plato, his disciple, created a more famous school of our time, the Academy, the true and proper center of thought, and challenge to the government and politics based mainly on opinion.

At the beginning of our civilization, in fact, when the problem of truth rose and became explicit and the search for it began, it became a philosophy with the participation of the community. Plato explains that philosophy is like a flame which is lit in the soul of the individual only after a long period of communal life and discussion, only after a true and real school of life and thought where philosophers would live together. The idea of truth itself is born from a common heritage and becomes incomprehensible at the moment in which it is understood as a testimony of the individual or of a separate group.

The first philosophical community founded by Plato in fact is a role model for future groups and societies who seriously intend to pursue the query of truth. St. Charles Preparatory School is above all your academy in which you discover the truth with the participation of a community in the context of a creative fraternity or brotherhood among yourselves, among the 570 or 580 students you are here.

Fraternity is the third ring, just like the coat of arms of Borromeo. It allows you to unite integrity and truth, and without this fraternity, integrity and truth would fall apart. You may remember the famous trilogy of the French Revolution: liberty, equality, and fraternity. Well, liberty and equality have deeply influenced the political history of peoples leading to the enrichment of civilization and creating such conditions that the dignity of the human person could be better expressed. Liberty and equality have become juridical principles and are applied every day as general political categories. But if liberty only is emphasized it can become the privilege of the strongest, as we well know. If equality only is emphasized then as history has shown it can result in mass collectivism.

So how can this truth, once acquired, be brought to fruition? The key seems to lie in giving fraternity its proper place among sources and political categories. Only if each of the three principles is given its proper importance can they give rise to social and international relations that can meet the challenges of today's world. And by experience we can say the same of the trilogy: integrity, truth, and fraternity. Fraternity is somehow the missing link, the missing ring that hinders us from discerning the truth and a true holiness. The lack of it hinders us from discerning the truth and achieving holiness. Originality, freshness and effectiveness in our daily mutual relations as well as in the source of political and international realm appear possible by means of fraternity of brother-hood.

Integrity and truth form an inseparable trilogy along with fraternity. The title of our conversation today is the most searched words from integrity to truthiness. What's next exactly? I would dare to say next is fraternity, and this is the wish I have for you all today: that you may experience and establish day after day more fraternity among you. And this will be the ring in the coat of arms of this school that paves the way for clarity of mind to determine and under-stand the truth and it will pave the way for which the sense of personal and social holiness.

- March 2, 2007

A native of Cuneo, in the Piedmont region of Italy, His Excellency **ARCHBISHOP CELESTINO MIGLIORE** *was born on July 1, 1952. He was ordained a priest on June 25, 1977.*

Archbishop Migliore obtained a master's degree in theology at the Center of Theological Studies in Fossano. He then pursued his studies at the Pontifical Lateran University, where he was awarded the Doctorate in Canon Law. In 1980, after graduating from the Pontifical Academy for Ecclesiastical Diplomacy, he joined the Holy See's diplomatic service.

His first assignment was to Angola, where, from 1980 to 1984 he served as attaché and second secretary to the Apostolic Delegation. From there, he was transferred to the Apostolic Nunciature in the United States of America, where he served also as Alternate Observer to the Organization of American States. In 1988 he was appointed to the Apostolic Nunciature in Egypt, remaining there for a year. He was then assigned at the Apostolic Nunciature in Warsaw, Poland, a post he held until his appointment on April 14, 1992, as Special Envoy with the role of Permanent Observer of the Holy See to the Council of Europe in Strasbourg, France.

From December 1995 to October 2002, he served as Undersecretary of the Section for Relations with States of the Secretariat of State, at the Vatican. During his term, he was also in charge of fostering relations with several Asian countries that do not yet have formal diplomatic relations with the Holy See. In this capacity, he traveled to Beijing, Hanoi, and Pyongyang as Head of Delegation of the Holy See.

From July 9 to 20, 2001, Archbishop Migliore led the Delegation of the Holy See to the United Nations Conference on Illicit Trade in Small Arms and Light Weapons in All Its Aspects, held in New York. He also represented the Holy See at numerous other conferences, symposia and panels held in various European capitals on issues related to the World Trade Organization, the Economic Commission for Europe, the European Union and the Middle East.

While in Rome, he also taught Ecclesiastical Diplomacy at the Pontifical Lateran University as a Visiting Professor.

On October 30, 2002, His Holiness Pope John Paul II nominated Archbishop Migliore as Apostolic Nuncio and Permanent Observer of the Holy See to the United Nations, in New York. Archbishop Migliore is the fourth Permanent Observer of the Holy See, after Monsignor Giovannetti and Cardinals Cheli and Martino.

6

Rev. John I. Jenkins, C.S.C.

on

Service and Solidarity in Education

"An adult life that is solely in pursuit of one's own self-interest is in the end no more worthwhile than a child's game and probably a lot less satisfying. An education directed to the service of one's self does not bring a person to completeness."

I t's a tremendous honor for me to be here at St. Charles with all of you giving the Borromean Lecture this year. You've had some very distinguished lecturers in the past, Cardinal Theodore McCarrick, Cardinal Avery Dulles and Archbishop Celestino Migliore, the Apostolic Nuncio to the United Nations. It's a very distinguished list of people. And your ability to track these people to St. Charles is due, no doubt, to the great reputation of this school and to the great reputation of so many graduates of this school. You just heard from the St. Charles graduate that I know best, Dick Notebaert, a member of your 1965 class and chair of our board.

As it was said, Dick was a man who left St. Charles,

went to the University of Wisconsin, began in a company washing trucks, and ended up as its CEO. But more importantly he has been an extraordinarily generous supporter of so many organizations and good causes. And he is a man dedicated above all else to his family.

Last night I had the great opportunity to meet Bob Walter, Dominic Cavello, and Tom O'Leary, and they too exhibit the same great character and values that Dick has. If a measure of a school's greatness is the quality of its graduates, and if these men are at all typical of the graduates that St. Charles produces, then you, St. Charles students, are very privileged because you're attending a truly great school. And that privilege carries with it an obligation, an obligation to live up those standards, to be leaders, and to give back to your communities, to organizations, to the church.

Looking at this school, touring around here today, meeting so many of you, it struck me how similar this institution is to my institution, the University of Notre Dame; and not only because of our strong athletic teams. By the way, congratulations state swimming champs. Go Cardinals!

On a more substantial level, I think Notre Dame and St. Charles are alike because as Catholic institutions both are committed to guiding their educational efforts to educate the whole person, the individual in all his—and in our case, all her—dimensions: intellectual, moral, spiritual, and physical. I think the majority of educational institutions today don't have that broad commitment of educating the whole person. They tend to leave the middle of those four qualities, the moral and spiritual, to the care and attention of others or to the students themselves.

I think what makes Notre Dame and St. Charles so important and distinctive is that they differ. I noted in the St. Charles philosophy and belief statement—it was even in bold face—the following statement: "St. Charles finds its definition as a Catholic school and its dedication to develop, nurture and instill the gospel of Christ in the minds and lives of its students." There's nothing hands off or arms length about that statement and that ideal, and that's good thing.

You know, the founder of my religious community, Holy Cross, was a man recently beatified, Blessed Father Moreau, and he was French priest who sent another young French priest to the wilderness of Indiana in 1842 to found a school. And when he sent him he gave him a charge, to make it a school that educated not just the minds of its students but also their characters, their souls, with instruction in faith and including with physical training and, in those days, hard physical labor. Education, Moreau said, was the art of bringing a young person to completeness.

I noticed a banner today in the halls: holiness is wholeness. It's that same ideal–that same ideal that has guided Notre Dame throughout its 166 years of existence and continues today–and I've seen that it guides St. Charles in its 85th year that it has remained committed to the mission that Bishop James Hartley established for the school in 1923. Notre Dame and St. Charles are alike in another way. I think we share a commitment to serve our fellow human beings as an essential part of the educational process. Again, I quote your philosophy and belief statement: "As an authentic Christian community, the St. Charles family must be ordered to the service of others, to one another and to the community at large."

At Notre Dame, service has always been a part of our student's lives. Over 80 percent of our students engage in volunteer service. Ten percent each year will go on for a year of service, whether it's teaching in Catholic schools, whether it's working in South Bend, whether it's going across the ocean to serve in foreign nations; it has always been a part of the education at Notre Dame, and I can see it has been a part of the education at St. Charles. We do these things, of course, not so we can think about them, but we do them because they're part of the Christian life. Part of our tradition as Catholics, is to serve those who are less well off as believers in the gospel of Jesus Christ, as people sent by Christ to serve those in need.

Since all of St. Charles students take at least two years of Latin, I'm sure most of you know that the word education comes from a Latin word *educare*, meaning 'to lead a person out.' We in education must always ask ourselves: What are we leading young people out from and what are we leading them to? At one level I think the answers are simple: we're leading them out from ignorance to knowledge, out of confusion into wisdom and understanding. But maybe there's more to it than that.

I'm reminded of a line in *The Confessions of St. Augustine*, one of the greatest books ever written. I'm sure all of you St. Charles students have read or will read soon. In that book, Augustine is telling the story of his life and he reflects on his education as a young person and what it was like, and he's critical of it. He studies many of the same subjects you studied and he excelled in school, but at the beginning of that book he writes of his education as a young boy: "As a student, our teachers punished for playing boys' games. But this was not just, for they were teaching us to play adult games of seeking wealth and prestige, and that is not any more worthwhile than the games of boys."

I think Augustine has a profound insight there. An adult life that is solely in pursuit of one's own self-interest is in the end no more worthwhile than a child's game and probably a lot less satisfying. An education directed to the service of one's self does not bring a person to completeness. An education that teaches a person to measure success or happiness by that kind of standard is an education that leads us out of darkness into blindness. It leads us out of ignorance into what is in the end a dead end.

Where would real education lead us from and lead us to? I think at the heart of the University of Notre Dame and at the heart of St. Charles is a profound truth that it leads us to a paradox, the kind of paradox that allows us to find salvation in the Cross of Jesus Christ, an instrument of death and torture, but an instrument that leads to the resurrection and to life. And that's precisely the paradox Jesus was talking about when he said, "It is in giving that we receive, it is in dying that we're born to eternal life."

I hope you, St. Charles students, have discerned some of the mystery of that statement in your experience as a result of some of your service activities you've engaged in here at St. Charles Prep. I hope you have a sense of solidarity and satisfaction when you're joined together to collect food for the needy, to offer help and support to someone who has suffered loss or grief. That sense of solidarity with others of knowing that you have contributed in some way to easing the pain of another, to supporting them in difficult times, that is more satisfying than all the accomplishments in the world. You, students of St. Charles, are truly blessed to be here in an atmosphere of Christian love and commitment, an atmosphere where the wisdom of the paradox that Christ uttered can almost be taken for granted. It is in giving that we receive, it's in dying that we're born into eternal life.

Someday, when you're adults living and working in the larger American society, you will understand how uncommon this atmosphere is and how very lucky you are to be a student at St. Charles Prep. And if you have become the kind of leaders your teachers and mentors want you to be, you may have the opportunity to change things someway, to create an atmosphere in your neighborhood or in your work place that will reflect to some degree what you're experiencing now at the school at St. Charles Prep. And I pray that when that day comes, when you hear that call, you will like Samuel in the Bible story, simply turn and say, "Here I am, Lord, send me."

We will expect a lot of you. After all, you're St. Charles grads. We have a right to expect a lot of you and we look for you to be the leaders of the future. Thank you for this great honor of addressing you at this great school. Thank you for all you stand for and all you accomplish and thank you for listening to me today. God bless you all.

- February 28, 2008

REV. JOHN I. JENKINS, C.S.C. *became the 17th president of the University of Notre Dame on July 1, 2005, and began a second five-year term in July 2010. He had previously served from 2000-04 as vice president and associate provost.*

Father Jenkins has continued his call for civil discourse in our nation – grounded in the Christian view of others as equally made in the image of God – as a way to find common ground rather than demonize those with a different opinion. In a speech at Emory University in 2011, he said: "If we choose to attack our opponents before we have taken the time to understand them, if we prefer denunciations to genuine dialogue, if we seek political victory rather than constructive compromise…we will not be able to find solutions to the problems before us." The Commission on Presidential Debates, a non-partisan, non-profit organization that sponsors and produces all U.S. presidential and vice presidential debates, cited his leadership on this issue in electing him to its board of directors in 2011.

A Notre Dame alumnus, Father Jenkins earned bachelor's and master's degrees in philosophy from the University in 1976 and 1978, respectively, and was ordained a priest of the Congregation of Holy Cross in the Basilica of the Sacred Heart on campus in 1983. While earning bachelor's and doctoral degrees in philosophy from Oxford University in 1987 and 1989, respectively, he also taught in Notre Dame's London Undergraduate Program. He earned a master of divinity degree and licentiate in sacred theology from the Jesuit School of Theology at Berkeley in 1988.

A member of the Notre Dame philosophy faculty since 1990 and the recipient of a Lilly Teaching Fellowship in

1991-92, Father Jenkins served as director of the Old College program for Holy Cross seminarians from 1991 to 1993, and as religious superior of the Holy Cross priests and brothers at Notre Dame from 1997 to 2000. He is the author of numerous scholarly articles published in The Journal of Philosophy, Medieval Philosophy and Theology, and The Journal of Religious Ethics, and of the book, Knowledge and Faith in Thomas Aquinas.

Father Jenkins is a recipient of the Ellis Island Medal of Honor, which is given to those showing outstanding qualities in their personal and professional lives, yet maintaining the richness of their particular heritage. He also holds honorary degrees from Benedictine College (2006), the University of San Francisco (2010) and Aquinas College (2011), and was the 2009 recipient of the American Irish Historical Society's Gold Medal. In 2010, he was elected a member of the American Academy of Arts and Sciences, an association honoring leading "thinkers and doers" since the 18th century, and in 2011 he was appointed to the academy's Commission on the Humanities and Social Sciences, which aims to bolster teaching and research in these disciplines. He also received a Champion of Diversity Award from Indiana Minority Business Magazine in 2011. He is a member of the Association of Catholic Colleges and Universities Board of Directors and a past chair of the Big East Conference Presidents and Chancellors Committee.

7

Carl A. Anderson

on
Building a Civilization of Love

*"Are we willing to make that kind of commitment, to do
what we can to move forward and to help others who
are in need of what we can provide, as Americans, and
as Catholics?"*

I'm very grateful for the opportunity to be with
you today to give this annual lecture in honor of
St. Charles Borromeo, especially this year since
it's the 470th anniversary of his birth. He is also my
Patron Saint, and any time you get the opportunity to
give a lecture in honor of your patron saint you better
seize the opportunity. I think all of you know that St.
Charles was one of the great saints in the history of
the Catholic Church. He did so much to change the
history of the Catholic Church, and one of the most
interesting things about St. Charles Borromeo is that
he was appointed a Cardinal at age 22, and made Secretary of State of the Vatican, and Governor of the

Papal States. Now, a cynic might say, "Well, that's what happens when your uncle happens to be Pope during the Renaissance." But Renaissance popes tended to have large families, and they all wanted jobs. So what made Charles Borromeo so special? The same reason that makes him so special for you. The pope saw in Charles Borromeo a man who had already formed his character in an outstanding way and who was capable of outstanding leadership by age 22. This meant that when he was your age he was already making decisions that were shaping his character and shaping his life.

Now one of the things that people who are speaking to students on occasions like this do is to remind you that you are the future. Society takes a great interest in you because you are tremendously valuable to the future of society. Because you are important to the future of society, your parents and others are investing a lot in you so that in the future you can make a contribution to society. But that should not obscure the fact that the decisions you make today are some of the most important decisions that you will make in your life, because like St. Charles the decisions you are making today are forming not only the person who you will become but also the person who you are now. And that is why there was a popular saying in the classical world that the child is the father of the man.

I have been asked to speak today on the topic of my recent book, "A Civilization of Love," and you might ask – "Building a civilization of love - isn't that kind of a strange topic for someone who's leading an organization of 1.7 million men?" The idea which was promoted by Pope John Paul II and now by Pope Benedict XVI is a very simple one. The idea is that the great Christian commandment – to love one's neighbor, and to treat your neighbor as you would want to be treated – ought to be the operating principle of society. That ought to be the principle on which we not only live our private lives, but also the basis upon which we treat each other in our public lives. You may ask, "What kind of difference would that make?" Well, I think all of us have been watching what has been happening with the economy, the financial markets, during the last couple of months. Certainly your parents have been watching. And you have to ask yourself, would those kinds of difficulties have occurred if the people making those decisions had real care and concern for the people whose investments they were in charge of stewarding. If they were treating their neighbor as they would want to have been treated, would they have made the kind of economic decisions that have caused so many thousands of families to lose their homes, to lose their jobs, and to threaten their security and their future? So I think the pope was on to something very important when he said that as Christians we have a fundamental responsibility to live our life based on the fundamental value, love of neighbor, which is a fundamental message of Christianity.

The longer I work in the Knights of Columbus – and I have been Supreme Knight since 2000 –
the more I've come in contact with some great men,
and these men have impressed me with the truth of
this message. I think the first group that I met the
first year that I was Supreme Knight were many of
the fire fighters of 9/11. We all know their story; we
all know their heroism; we all know what they did in
New York City that day. But we should not think of
those men as having just performed their duty. They
had performed their duty, and they were told to leave
those buildings. They had done everything that was
reasonably expected of them – all that their duty required that they do. But they didn't leave those buildings. They continued their work. They continued to
go up those stairs. Why was that? Because they
loved their families less? To the contrary, I think it
was because they loved their families more. They understood the importance of what they were doing for
the families of those they were rescuing. And so I
think what motivated the heroes of 9/11 was not duty
but love; love for their neighbor.

Take a look at the men returning from duty in
Iraq, and from Afghanistan. I have met a lot of them.
I've met some in Veteran's Hospitals, where they are
being put back together again. And a lot of those
guys come back hurt because they stepped out of
their way to help a buddy, or to help a civilian. They
went beyond duty. They went beyond what their responsibility called for them to do. And when you talk

to them – men who have lost an arm, lost a leg, they want to go back to Iraq and Afghanistan to serve. It is not only duty, it is for love of country, love for the people they are defending, love for their colleagues.

Take a look at some of the great sports figures – we've got a lot of them in the Knights of Columbus. I have gotten to meet a few. When we consider real champions, how do we describe them? Look at a quarterback. He stays in the pocket, right? He knows that a defensive lineman is coming, and may hit him hard, yet he stays there. When we look at great athletes, what do we say? We say they have a love for the game. What distinguishes them above the others? They have great heart. They have not just talent. They have something extra. So what I have concluded is that the vocation to love that we hear about as Christians, that the popes have talked about so much recently, is really a very masculine value, and a very manly virtue. That's a lesson that I've learned by working with a number of men who I consider to be real heroes. And this is consistent with the Bible. Consider Scripture John 3:16, "God so loved the world that He sent his only son." God the Father (from whom all fathers take their name) so loved the world He sent his only son. And the son responds out of love for the father to save the world. So, love is the motivating principle. If you want to know what is the most masculine virtue, it's an authentic vocation to love of neighbor, that is expressed eternally in the relationship between the Father and the Son.

I mentioned 9/11 in the context of this idea of a civilization of love. Every year the pope issues a message for the World Day of Prayer for Peace. And I would encourage any of you who are interested to go back and read Pope John Paul II's message for the World Day of Prayer for Peace in January 2001. What he asked Christians around the globe to pray for in January 2001 was greater understanding, cooperation and tolerance among the world's great religions. And he concluded that statement by recalling World Youth Day, and recalling how many times he asked young men and women to become engaged in building a new civilization, a new culture – what he called the Civilization of Love. He said that each of you has that high calling. The most important foundation to that is what we would call the theological virtues – faith, hope, charity – precisely the three virtues that Pope Benedict XVI has chosen for his two great encyclicals, *Deus Caritas Est* and *Spe Salvi*. Faith, hope, charity. As Knights of Columbus, we do a lot of work in that regard. Looking at our founder 125 years ago, a young priest – 27 years old – took the principles charity, unity, fraternity, and built a men's organization upon them. He didn't have the benefit of a pope who was talking about building a civilization of love, so he came up with principles that he thought would motivate the men of his day to accomplish the same purpose: to protect their families, to strengthen their communities, and to reach out and help those in need. That's the great challenge that is being presented to each of us, but especially being presented to the young men in this school who have been given so many opportunities.

It was mentioned earlier that I've recently returned from participating in the World Synod of Bishops where there were bishops from around the world – bishops from countries in which Christians are persecuted and killed, like Pakistan and India – countries in which Christians do not have the freedom to meet like we meet, countries in which Christians don't have the opportunity to go to church safely on Sunday, and yet they have struggled for years to preserve their Christian identity and faith.

We have a tremendous opportunity, a tremendous responsibility, to do what so many others in the world cannot do. So the question is – Are we willing to make that kind of commitment, to do what we can to move forward and to help others who are in need of what we can provide, as Americans, and as Catholics? We have just gone through an extraordinary election in this country. People have voted overwhelmingly to move forward in a new direction around the ideas of hope and change. Christianity is a religion of hope, it is a religion of change, and it is a responsibility of those of us who take the name of Christian to make a contribution in that regard. And this is what people are going to be looking to you, as a graduate of this institution, with such a proud tradition.

I started off speaking of future and present,

but ideas of past, present and future are human limitations; they are not Divine limitations. When God looks at each of us, He sees our entire life at once. He sees all the decisions that we will make. He sees the direction our life will take, and what we will accomplish. And he knows the purpose for which each of us has been put here on this earth. He knows that each of us has a specific mission, and therefore each of us has a specific vocation. Mother Teresa used to say – and she used to say it to individuals like us, and she used to say it to bishops and cardinals – she used to say, "Give God permission." Give God permission to come into your life, and to change your life. And if you do that, you will never be disappointed. In fact, you will be able to accomplish something great in your life – great for your country, great for your community, great for your family, but most of all great for yourself.

And so that's basically what I wanted to say to you today – that each of you has a great opportunity here. You have been given things that people around the world cannot imagine the possibility of having. We may take it for granted, but we shouldn't, because not only do you have a great opportunity, you have an opportunity that is within your power to realize in a great way. And so I want to thank you for the privilege of being with you today, and being a part of this great tradition of St. Charles.

- November 6, 2008

As supreme knight of the Knights of Columbus, **CARL A. ANDERSON** *is the chief executive officer and chairman of the board of the world's largest Catholic family fraternal service organization, which has more than 1.8 million members.*

Mr. Anderson has had a distinguished career as a public servant and educator. From 1983 to 1987, he served in various positions of the Executive Office of the President of the United States, including special assistant to the President and acting director of the White House Office of Public Liaison. Following his service at the White House, Mr. Anderson served for nearly a decade as a member of the U.S. Commission on Civil Rights.

From 1983 to 1998, Mr. Anderson taught as a visiting professor of family law at the Pontifical John Paul II Institute for Studies on Marriage and Family at the Pontifical Lateran University in Rome. In 1988, he became the founding vice president and first dean of the Washington, D.C., session of this graduate school of theology now located at The Catholic University of America.

He is the author of the New York Times bestseller, A Civilization of Love: What Every Catholic Can Do To Transform The World; co-author (with Msgr. Eduardo Chávez) of Our Lady of Guadalupe: Mother of the Civilization of Love, also a New York Times bestseller; co-editor (with Livio Melina) of The Way of Love: Reflections on Pope Benedict XVI's Encyclical Deus Caritas Est; (with José Granados) Called to Love: Approaching John Paul II's Theology of the Body; and Beyond a House Divided: The Moral Consensus Ignored by Washington, Wall Street & the Media.

Mr. Anderson was the only Catholic layman from North America to serve as an auditor at the World Synod of Bishops in 2001, 2005 and 2008.

Pope John Paul II appointed Mr. Anderson as a member of the Pontifical Academy for Life (1998) and the Pontifical Council for the Laity (2002), and as a consultor to the Pontifical Council for Justice and Peace (2003). Pope Benedict XVI appointed him as a consultor to the Pontifical Council for Social Communications (2007) and as a member of the Pontifical Council for the Family (2008). He is a member of the Board of Superintendence of the (I.O.R.) (Institute for the Works of Religion - Vatican Bank) (2009) and has served as a consultant to the Pro-Life Committee of the U.S. Conference of Catholic Bishops (USCCB) since 2002.

Mr. Anderson is a Knight Grand Cross of the Order of St. Sylvester; a Knight of the Order of St. Gregory the Great; and a Knight Grand Cross of the Order of the Holy Sepulchre of Jerusalem.

He serves as a member of the International Scientific Council of the Studium Generale Marcianum of Venice. In 1994, he was a member of the Vatican delegation for the Fifteenth Meeting of the International Jewish Liaison Committee, held in Jerusalem.

Mr. Anderson currently serves on the Board of Trustees of The Catholic University of America and the Basilica of the National Shrine of the Immaculate Conception. He has received honorary doctorates from The Catholic University of America, The Pontifical Theology Academy of Krakow and St. Vincent's Seminary, Latrobe, Pa. Mr. Anderson is the recipient of many honors, including the Imago Dei Award, Archdio-

cese of Denver (2005); the Canterbury Medal, Becket Fund for Religious Liberty (2007); Servant of Peace Award, Path to Peace Foundation (2007); Rector's Award, Pontifical North American College, Rome (2008); The John Carroll Society Award (2009); the Lupa Capitolina Award, City of Rome (2009); and the John Cardinal O'Connor Award (2009).

In over a decade as the chief executive officer of the Order, Anderson has overseen strong growth in the Knights' financial resources — many of which have nearly doubled during his tenure. Life insurance in force has doubled from $40.4 billion to approximately $82 billion — an increase of nearly 7 percent a year. Annual life insurance sales have also increased — from $4.0 billion in 2000 to $7.77 billion in 2010 — an annual growth rate of 6.8 percent.

Mr. Anderson holds degrees in philosophy from Seattle University and law from the University of Denver. He is a member of the bar of the District of Columbia and is admitted to practice law before the U.S. Supreme Court.

He and his wife, Dorian, are the parents of five children.

8

Rev. Robert F. O'Toole, S.J.

on
The Sacred Scriptures and Civility

"Personally, I have never been very satisfied by the adage, 'Agree to disagree.' I guess like many I am convinced that the truth is there and through reasoning together in a civil and courteous manner we should be able to arrive at it."

Who can deny the lack of civility today? In the presence of the entire Congress, Representative Joe Wilson shouted at President Obama, "You lie." In the semi-finals of the U.S. Open, Serena Williams, and in the finals, Roger Federer, both had discourteous meltdowns, and who was not shocked when Kanye West took the microphone from Taylor Swift to promote his favorite, Beyoncé? Even religious concerns, though they might well be quite valid, are not always handled civilly.

In addressing the question of civility, we do best to start with a description of the reality in which we find ourselves; at the same time, let's be reflecting about the reasons for this lack of civility. There are reasons to be upset and angry. Terrorism has entered our lives and led to the deaths of thousands of people and war on two fronts. Nor are we really sure that Islam is open to religious and civil tolerance or to a mutual respect and esteem of others and their religious traditions. Presently the media is telling us that we are out of the recession, but the global financial crisis is still affecting everyone, especially the poor.

Moreover, are we really out of the recession? Neighbors, friends and even family members have seen their investments and retirement funds lose as much as 30 percent or more of their value; true, the market has improved, but the recovery is just getting under way. At the end of August, the jobless rate in the U.S. was 9.7 percent. The housing market has improved, but the government stimulus plan is coming to an end, and we do not know if it will be extended. California, New Jersey and other states had significant problems in passing their fiscal budgets, for their revenues could not cover their expenditures. Since 2007 the FDIC has seized 70 banks. Perhaps the most irritating reality is that the majority of those who caused the world's financial problems have shown no remorse for their failure and are now even benefiting financially from the various national and other efforts at recovery. Likewise discouraging is the reality that the problems with the structural issues with American high finance are still there; a program of real reform is needed to restore full confidence and ensure a system that works for all levels of the economy. So, let's admit it; it is no surprise that people are on edge; in fact, our present age has been described as "the age of rage."

Are today's comedians on TV a mirror on our society? There is little self-deprecating humor or wholesome humor due to creative and patient study of the inconsistencies and funny aspects of human life, but rather denigrating and crude abuse of others and their weaknesses, or supposed ones.

Fortunately, the vast majority of people do not want to be dominated by even these hard financial times and challenges or to revel in a lack of esteem and appreciation of others, for all that is achieved by so doing is a lack of esteem for ourselves and disappointment in failing to be the kind of persons we should be.

Thanks to those who have been influential in our lives, we know that there is a better way of responding to these challenges and of being civil, courteous and polite to everyone we encounter. This civility calls for a true respect and a growing trust in the other person and an appreciation of his or her point of view even though we see it as erroneous and far from the truth.

Our Catholic, Christian stance toward the other finds its roots in the Bible message. Surely the Sacred Scriptures were written centuries ago and the expectations of how human beings were to interact with one another were different and not as refined as we think they should be today. Nonetheless, the civility which most of us treasure and view as essential for peaceful and efficient interaction in society flows from the Bible's message. Also, although the Bible is concerned about religious truths, the principles that it offers can be applied to civility in our personal and professional lives.

We are told in the Old Testament that we human beings, both male and female, are created in God's image and likeness (Gen 1:27); each human being has an inherent dignity which comes from God himself. So, looking down on anyone or failing to appreciate how God is in him or her isn't the right approach. Rather, in the back of our minds we hear St. Matthew's description of the last judgment of the nations, of everyone, and how what we do to the least of our brothers and sisters we do to Jesus (25:31-46). This portrayal of the last judgment should come to us as no surprise since our main commands are to love God and our neighbor. Love of one another was Jesus' command, and he could say of himself, "There is no greater love than this: to lay down one's life for one's friend." There is no reason why we should not see our discussion-partner as a friend. Even if we might hesitate, for one reason or another, in doing that, seeing the image of God in the other and listening to Jesus' call to love still direct what our stance toward any dialogue-partner should be. This being the case, courtesy, thoughtfulness and good manner, that is civility, should characterize all of our interactions with others.

Theoretically, in a discussion all the participants are seeking the truth and want to do what is right. Perhaps, one of the most impressive characteristics of Catholicism is that we are committed to be faithful to our religious tradition but at the same time are determined to remain open to the whole of creation so that we move toward the total truth God is communicating to us. We are all willing to say "Amen" to that; however, isn't it true that we all come to a discussion or argument shaped by our numerous experiences of life? Hopefully, most of this shaping has been positive; but honestly, we know that is not totally true of who we are as we enter a civil discussion with someone. Everyone brings baggage, but not everyone is aware of the baggage he or she bringing. Of course, it is always easier to determine the baggage that our dialogue partner or partners have; but until we have reached an accepting and mutually respectful relationship, there is not much that we can do about that. On the other hand, we can do quite a bit about trying to get in touch with the negative baggage, even prejudices, that we are bringing to the discussion. It takes humility and courage to deal with one's negative baggage; once we have done so, we are much more honest dialogue partners. If I am unwilling to do so, St. Matthew (7:5) has some strong words for us, "You hypocrite! Remove the plank from your own eye first, then you will see clearly to take the speck from your brother's or sister's eye."

Not only should we be willing to listen carefully

to our dialogue partner; it can prove most helpful to civility to work at understanding the other's position. The old adage is, "Don't judge the other until you have walked a mile in his or her shoes," ok, "moccasins." Our effort to do so immediately gives us some distance from the position that we may be defending most vigorously and provides a different perspective from which to consider what the other is thinking and why. There is no guarantee that we will be won over to his or her position, but it might well create in us a healthy and compassionate stance toward the other that will certainly improve the relationship we are establishing with them. Paul has something to say on this point, and his words to the Philippians are particularly striking:

"Never act out of rivalry or conceit; rather, let all parties think humbly of others as superior to themselves, each of you looking to the others' interests rather than to his own. Your attitude should be that of Christ, Though he was in the form of God, he did not deem equality with God something to be grasped at. Rather he emptied himself and took the form of a slave" (2:3-7)

Please do not misunderstand me; I am not advocating that civility demands of us that we do not try to establish the truth. On the contrary, in any discussion we should make every effort to arrive at the truth; what I am claiming is that we should do this in a polite and civil manner. The odds are that if we try to arrive at the truth in a very aggressive and offensive manner, our possibility of getting there is lessened considerably. However, situations can become quite complicated and what we are not able to achieve in one context, we might be able to do in another.

Let's take an example from Paul, who very forcefully interacted with Peter at Antioch in Syria. Without any attention to the Jewish dietary laws Peter was eating with Jewish and Gentile Christians; however, certain individuals came from James, Jesus' relative, his cousin, and arrived at Antioch. This led Peter and the other Jewish Christians to stop eating with the Gentile Christians and to eat by themselves. Paul was upset with Peter because his behavior was not true to the truth of the gospel and interacted with him in a very strong manner, and even speaks of the hypocrisy of the Jewish Christians. Paul says to Peter, "If you are a Jew living according to Gentile ways rather than Jewish ways, by what logic do you force the Gentiles to adopt Jewish ways" (Gal 2:14, cf. vv. 11-14).

In this brief but compelling interaction, you may think that Paul was not particularly civil with Peter. The times were different, and different civil behavior was part of the culture, but please do not judge this interaction too rapidly; for if you are a Christian and your mother is not Jewish, Paul is arguing for you. You and I would have been second-class Christians who were not permitted to eat with the first-class Jewish Christians unless we kept the Jewish dietary laws. Paul recognized that such behavior was not true to the gospel message and that Peter's behavior was not logically consistent. Our challenge is to represent the truth as best we can, but to do so in a way that is civilly and socially acceptable to modern times and to how Christians should interact with others, today.

One New Testament writer is concerned that the Church work out its disagreements in a civil and peaceful manner and provide examples of this. I am speaking of St. Luke, who wrote both his Gospel and the Acts of the Apostles. His main example of this is in the Acts of the Apostles, chapter 15. One of the major questions facing the early Church was how should Gentile Christians be allowed to enter the Church. We have already considered the question of the observance of the Jewish dietary laws, but an even more important discussion related to circumcision. Many Jewish Christians were convinced that Gentiles had to be circumcised in order to become Christians and were teaching this, So, Paul and Barnabas went up to Jerusalem to get this matter settled by the whole Church. Peter speaks first and points out at the end of his speech to those gathered in the house of centurion Cornelius that God showed his approval of the Gentiles entering the Christian community without being circumcised by granting them the Holy Spirit just as he had done to the Jews at Pentecost. So, God made no distinction between the Gentiles Christians and Jewish ones, but through faith purified the hearts of both. James, Jesus' cousin and the then-head of the Jerusalem church, explains that Peter's words agree with the words of the prophets and complies with the directive that the Gentile Christians are to be asked only to abstain from anything contaminated by idols, that is, offered to idols, illicit sexual unions, the meat of strangled animals and eating blood, but nothing further. The assembled Christians agreed with this decision, and a letter to this effect is sent to the church in Antioch. Luke pictures a courteous, polite and mutually respectful discussion of the problem and of what God and the prophets have revealed about the matter, and how the Christian community can address such an important question in a loving and fraternal manner and hit upon a solution which will prove agreeable to everyone concerned. Luke's implication is that when in the future the Church addresses similar important questions, its members do as was done at this meeting.

Even though our experience may be somewhat limited, we are all aware that discussions do not always flow so smoothly. When we feel that we have been treated unjustly in a discussion, there is the natural tendency to get even, to even go back to the early Jewish law of "An eye for an eye, a tooth for a tooth." However, St. Matthew (5:38-42) cites Jesus as saying "But what I say to you is: Offer no resistance to injury. When a person strikes you on the right cheek, turn and offer him the other. If anyone wants to go to law over your shirt, hand him also your coat as well." Jesus calls us to a stance toward our neighbor, our dialogue partner, which obviously cannot be easily achieved; but his directive has more possibility of advancing our discussion than does getting even, which will not bring about a better and more accurate exchange of ideas but rather make enemies.

Personally, I have never been very satisfied by the adage, "Agree to disagree." I guess like many I am convinced that the truth is there and through reasoning together in a civil and courteous manner we should be able to arrive at it. During the recent presidential election, I was involved in a truly vigorous debate with my four living sisters. The topic was: Should one vote in a presidential election considering one issue, no matter how important it may be, as the deciding factor or not? I was strongly against such a position, and the discussion went back and forth for months. Neither side gave much ground, actually any ground; fortunately, my seven living brothers were not involved in the discussion. Finally I had to write my sisters, "Let's agree to disagree on the matter." We did not arrive at the ideal, determining what the real truth was or winning the other over to our opinion. However, through our polite, courteous and sometimes vigorous exchange of ideas we achieved what is perhaps the greatest benefit of civility, our respect and esteem for each other and a more profound appreciation of the integrity of each of us in dealing with an extremely important question. Our civility was a recognition of the image of God and the presence of Christ in each other and a living out of the command of loving thy neighbor.

Today, we face many difficult challenges, but being civil is the best way to address them and carries out the biblical message.

- October 13, 2009

REV. ROBERT F. O'TOOLE, S.J., *was born and raised in St. Louis and entered the Jesuit order in 1954. He completed his doctorate in Sacred Scriptures at the Pontifical Biblical Institute in Rome; his director was the then-Father Carlo Maria Martini, S.J., later Cardinal-Archbishop of Milan. He holds an M.A. in Greek and Latin.*

Father O'Toole taught at St. Louis University for 17 years and in 1991 moved to the Biblical Faculty at the Pontifical Biblical Institute, where he was also Superior of the community and then Rector of the Institute.

In September of 2003, he was named the President of the Gregorian University Foundation.

In 2002, he completed six years as the Rector of the Pontifical Biblical Institute, where he received his Licentiate and Doctorate, and where he has been a professor since 1991. Before that he was a theology professor at St. Louis University, his alma mater, where he earned a Bachelor's in Philosophy and Letters, a Licentiate in Philosophy and a Masters in Classical Languages and taught from 1974 to 1991.

Father O'Toole has published extensively. Father O'Toole authored the books: The Christological Climax of Paul's Defense, The Unity of Luke's Theology: An Analysis of Luke-Acts, and Who Is a Christian? A Study in Pauline Ethics. He also has written dozens of scholarly articles for many publications.

9

Rev. Jeffrey von Arx, S.J.

on
The Nature and Future of Civility

*"To be civil then, is to have adopted a mode of conduct,
and inherent in that mode of conduct is respect for the
laws and conventions that recognize the dignity of others
so that we may live together with one another in a state of
mutual felicity."*

Samuel Johnson, the great 18th century English critic and the compiler of the first English dictionary somewhat offhandedly defined "Civility" as: "the state of being civilized: freedom from barbarity."

It's not a particularly expansive definition, but it certainly covers the essentials. First of all, civility is a "state," it is a disposition, an orientation. To be civil is to afford others a level of respect and dignity that you would wish for yourself; it is to prefer to engage in reasonable dialogue rather than to resort to violence or bullying in order to reach an agreement.

To be civil then, is to have adopted a mode of conduct, and inherent in that mode of conduct is respect for the laws and conventions that recognize the dignity of others so that we may live together with one another in a state of mutual felicity.

Civility is also—as Johnson points out—a kind of freedom, a freedom from barbarity. The rules of barbarity and the rules of civility are very different. The rule of barbarity is this: Basically, whoever has the most power, wins. When civility breaks down, what follows is social chaos—bloodshed, thievery, betrayal, you name it. We see this all the time. When one college roommate videotapes another college roommate and puts those images on the Internet in order to humiliate his roommate, we are witnessing the triumph of barbarity over civility, a barbarity that is not that far beneath the surface of civility most of the time.

So "civility" cannot be taken for granted; in fact, civility, as we understand it is not something that has always governed human affairs. It arises in the West as a virtue and an attribute to be admired at a very specific moment in our history.

As an historian, this is a matter of interest and concern to me. If civility—the freedom from barbarity—is a "state" that arises in a society out of a particular set of historical circumstances, then there is no guarantee that civility, as a virtue to be admired, will survive as historical circumstances change. At the very least, the notion of "civility" cannot be allowed to deteriorate into a static and empty set of rules, manners, or codes of etiquette, but must be actively and determinedly reinvigorated as historical circumstances change and our cultures evolve. We must continually rediscover the virtue of civility. That way, the freedom of barbarity that most of us enjoy will continue, and furthermore, we may be able to extend that freedom to those who have yet to enjoy it.

What I'd like to do today is to look forward toward the future, and ask some questions about what it might mean to be "civil" in the new world that we have recently entered, the world which has as its "principal new feature" what Pope Benedict XVI calls "the explosion of worldwide interdependence, commonly known as globalization."

But I'd like to begin by going back to another time of dramatic social change, innovation, and globalization—the era in which our idea of "civility" began to take shape. Roughly speaking, I'm talking about the 15th and 16th centuries, or the period that includes what we call the Renaissance, the Reformation, and the Counter-Reformation.

I want to share with you a bit of a letter written by Jean de Lannoy, a nobleman born about 1410, who served most of his life as an advisor to the Duke of Burgundy. At what was then the ripe old age of 54, Lannoy' s wife bore him a son, Louis. Knowing that he would not live long enough to be able to give his son any instruction, Jean de Lannoy decided to leave a letter to' be given to the boy when he was old enough to read it.

The basic message that the father conveys to the son is this: "For God' sake get an education—in particular, get a broad liberal arts education." That isn't precisely what he says but it certainly is the upshot. Here's an excerpt:

Those who have learned and retained much, and who have the greatest desire to learn and know, attain great good, honor and riches. This has often caused me displeasure not for envy of them but, because of my simplicity and slight knowledge and because I was never put to school. I therefore know and can know nothing. I realize that this chance is for me lost and gone, never to be recovered.... No day passes that I do not regret this, and especially when I find myself in the council of the king or of the Duke of Burgundy, and I know not nor dare not to speak my opinion after the learned, elegant [lawyers] and [historians] have spoken before me. For I do not know the order or manner of speaking and can say nothing ...Whence I have often felt deep shame and humiliation in my heart.

I find this letter deeply poignant. Here is a man from one age looking across a river that he will never cross, at a new age, seeing a world of ideas flowering on a distant shore, and knowing that it is a world in which he will play no part.

What had changed? At the time when the writer of this letter was born, Europe was still a late-Medieval society. It might not have been entirely barbarous, but it was pretty close. What held the social fabric together all over Europe were networks of fealty, kinship, and tribal loyalty.

The virtue that was most admired—where the governing classes were concerned at any rate—was prowess on the battlefield and power in general. So the qualities that were expressly admired in poetry and literature were physical courage, quickness to anger, sumptuous living, and passion. These networks of fealty were cemented by marriages, gifts of land, money, and titles. Education was at this period, in general, purely vocational. Clerics would go to university to learn Latin, medicine, or law for the purposes of serving as clerks in the bureaucracy of the Church or in court. But the idea of being educated for its own sake—as a matter of self-betterment or to increase one's capacity to make intelligent, persuasive conversation—would have been utterly foreign to Jean de Lannoy in his youth.

But within just a few decades, the world had been turned upside down. Christopher Columbus would soon reach the West Indies, and other explorers would open up new worlds for trade and exploration. Nicolaus Copernicus would establish that the earth was not the center of the solar system; Johannes Gutenberg had developed a printing system that would make books and therefore information and ideas, readily available. In fact by 1500, printing presses would print more than 20 million volumes— the greatest explosion in the dissemination of information in our culture's history, until the Internet.

Simultaneous with these discoveries and inventions would be a rediscovery of the works of Classical antiquity, and these Classical authors read in the original Greek would introduce novel ideas about what a society should be, what it meant to be a citizen, what was virtuous and desirable, and what was not. The rediscovery of the Greeks—their arts, poetry, history, and philosophy—was like discovering a treasure trove of lost ideas that were better and more intelligent than the ideas that had been floating around before, and it happened at a time when the economic and social fabric of Europe was loosening up.

To try and summarize the impact of this rediscovery would take us too long, but let's just say that, combined with the charitable traditions of Biblical Christianity, what was underway was a revolution in thinking about what a society should be and the emergence of the idea of the virtue of civility. The British Classical historian Gilbert Murray summarized the Greek influence on the thinking of the West this way: "an unquestioning respect for freedom of life and thought, a mistrust of passion ...a sure consciousness that the poor are fellow-citizens of the rich, and that statesmen must as a matter of fact consider the welfare of the whole state."

So, a very different set of values than those that poor Jean de Lannoy—who never went to school—grew up with.

What is also so wonderfully highlighted in this letter is how essential education is to civility. The young "lawyers" and "historians" who were now in ascendancy were men who were educated in Greek and Roman literature; they would have learned rhetoric—the art of speaking persuasively. They had acquired the tools that were necessary to be successful in this new age, and they had the "desire to know," a love of knowledge for its own sake, and the capacity to continue to learn, because they had acquired a cultivated mind. With that cultivated mind came the freedom to think, and speak, for themselves.

One figure who would be profoundly shaped by this shift in values from the culture of barbarity, to the culture of civility, was Ignatius Loyola, founder of the Society of Jesus, the religious order of which I am a member—and again, it is education that is at the heart of this transformation.

Ignatius, born in 1491, was, as you may know, a soldier—a Spanish nobleman from the Basque country who very much embraced the warrior culture as a young man. After being seriously wounded at the Battle of Pamplona in 1521, he recuperated at home and during his long and painful recuperation he turned to reading. A book on the life of Christ, *De Vita Christi*, had a profound effect on him—particularly the book's suggestion that the reader use their imagination to place himself in Christ's position. From here, Ignatius went on to read other books and was converted to a religious life.

But what kind of religious life? For the next 20 years, Ignatius would be a student, at first learning the basic grammatical and language skills that we would now consider a secondary education, and then going on to the University of Paris, where he studied philosophy and theology.

Along the way the nature of Ignatius vision of his own spiritual vocation would be transformed. What Ignatius came to appreciate was two things: That God was in effect educating him along the way, providing him with opportunities and challenges that expanded his mind and his understanding, and this he believed was true for everyone. God was the educator, par excellence, and what He taught us to do—if we were open to becoming educated—was to understand the nature of the world and respond to it in a truly authentic, and essentially civilized, way.

And second, Ignatius would come to see the importance of a religious life that reconciled nature and grace, human culture and religion. He would develop what is famously called a "world-friendly" spirituality, as opposed to the monastic and ascetic spiritualities that were characteristic of an earlier period.

The emphasis for Ignatius always, was "to help souls," and so as the Society of Jesus came into being, it was always oriented toward working with people in the conditions in which they found themselves in the world—as opposed to retreating from the world.

Indeed, one could say that Ignatian spirituality was a marriage between the traditions of Christian spirituality, and the world-embracing culture of civility that had displaced the warrior culture of Ignatius' youth.

The Society of Jesus got into the business of running schools almost by accident. In 1547, the city fathers of Messina in Sicily asked the Jesuits if they would open a school to teach their sons the basics— by which we mean the humanistic liberal arts, including Classical rhetoric, poetry, and drama—that were characteristic of the Renaissance grammar schools, and were believed to be uplifting to students, and of a benefit to the society at large. This mission was consistent with Ignatius's vision of an order that would "help souls" by educating them and preparing their minds for an encounter with the truth. Later, one of the early Jesuits would explain to King Philip ll of Spain that the reason the Jesuits believed in education as a religious mission was that "the proper education of the youth will mean improvement of the whole world."

In other words, educated persons will make the world a better place because they will naturally be inclined to improve the world around them, take leadership positions in society, and do so with the background in civility that a liberal arts education would give them. As another Jesuit contemporary, Juan Alfonso de Polanco would later elaborate: "Those who are now only students will grow up to be pastors, civic officials, administrators of justice, and will fill other important posts to everybody's profit and advantage."

Education was the rage in this period. St. Charles Borromeo—a contemporary of Ignatius—was deeply influenced by Jesuit pedagogy, and understood that a civilizing education was critical to the reformation of the Church. Among his many efforts that contributed to the modernization of the Church was the establishment of seminaries, colleges, and communities for the education of men entering holy orders. In effect, he too believed that the "proper education" of men entering the priesthood "would benefit the whole world," and that an educated clergy, imbued with the humanistic values of civility, was essential if the Church was to keep pace with the pace of intellectual and cultural change that characterized the age.

By 1773, the Society of Jesus would operate 800 educational institutions around the globe—the largest network of schools the world had ever seen. Many of these schools were established in the New World and in the Far East, areas that had only recently been able to be reached by Europeans. One of the distinguishing features of the early Jesuit missions to these regions was openness to the nature of these newly encountered cultures.

There's no question that the Jesuits believed it was their duty to spread the faith, but they also found that they learned so much about the nature of God, and the nature of men, by the profound differences they encountered in the cultures of what is now China, Japan, and India. This appreciation—that God is at work in every culture and that there is a limitless amount to learn about the truth through an openness to other cultures and their customs and languages—is without question a characteristic of those who have been educated in the liberal arts, by which I mean, those whose minds have been expanded through an encounter with other minds from other periods, and whose minds are supple enough to see the world through fresh eyes.

So civility, and education, go hand-in-hand. This is not to say that the more "educated" you are, the more civil you are, as anyone who works in a university can tell you. But it does mean that in general, to be open to the otherness of the other, to be able to listen and learn from what another person is saying without taking offence, to be able to be persuasive in argument, and tolerant of ambiguity and unresolved questions, are characteristics we acquire in general through an education that shapes our minds to perform in this manner.

So, what of the future? As I mentioned earlier, it seems clear that what we understand as "civility" is a "state" that arose in a particular period in our history, and in general, it has gone through modifications and, perhaps, degradations, but that tradition has continued to a large extent.

But there is no guarantee that it will continue. There are many positive dimensions to the "explosion of interdependence" that we have entered in the last few decades with the transformative impact of the Internet, the globalization of our economic institutions, the capacity for the instantaneous transmission of information, and so on. But these changes also present challenges.

In April of this year, in Mexico City, the Society of Jesus held a conference of Jesuit educators from close to 200 Jesuit-run universities and colleges from all over the world. At that time, the Superior General of the Society, Adolfo Nicolás, posed a set of challenges to all of us who work in Jesuit higher education. He asked us how we were going to educate young men and women to meet the challenges of this new, global century.

In effect, he asked us how we were going to continue the Jesuit tradition of educating young men and women to be "for others," in a way that took into account the currents and frictions of globalization.

At Fairfield University, where I am the President, we think a lot about these questions, and we see our mission as the education and formation of "global citizens," meaning young men and women who can operate freely across the boundaries of language and culture, who can think broadly across disciplines, and penetrate deeply into areas where they have no prior knowledge, because they have acquired the habits of mind—the intellectual rigor and the generosity of imagination—to be able to do so.

We are carrying on the Jesuit tradition of education, and adapting it as best we can to meet the challenges of our time.

What are these challenges, then? Well, Fr. Nicolás identified a number of them, but I'm going to focus on three of them that I believe pose tremendous challenges to the future of "civility" and our understanding of what it will mean to be a "civilized" person in the 21st century.

The first challenge is what Fr. Nicolás identified as the spread of two rival "isms,"by which he means aggressive secularism "that claims that faith has nothing to say to the world and its great problems (and which often claims that religion, in fact, is one of the world's great problems)" and on the other hand" the resurgence of various religious fundamentalisms" which "escape the complexity" of the world as it is today by taking refuge in a religious faith that is closed to dialogue, and "unregulated" by human reason.

In times of great stress and uncertainty, it is not unusual for groups that feel that they are marginalized or oppressed to take refuge in a belief system that insulates them from insecurity, so we must approach this kind of fundamentalism with understanding—and not with contempt.

And we have to understand that religious fundamentalisms are not necessarily primarily religious expressions at all, but are always interwoven with political and nationalist agendas and perspectives. As we encounter these fundamentalisms, as civilized persons, we need to be able to penetrate these distinctions and understand them—and not rush to judgment. That way, there is always the possibility of dialogue and shared understanding. We must not meet these fundamentalisms with a fundamentalism of our own.

At the same time, we need to make sure that the big, meaning-of-life questions that can only be encountered through spiritual reflection: "Why am I here?" Why is there something rather than nothing?" "What is it that I am called to discover about the world?" are not ridiculed or reduced to absurdity by the aggressive secularism that is so prevalent in many of our cultures. To me, the mark of a civilized person is their capacity to be comfortable standing a in a place of creative tension between what they can ascertain through reason and their apprehension of the mystery of Being that is beyond the confines of reason, or the confines of any particular religious expression.

So I think that to be "civil" in the future is to be one of those who can operate comfortably—without repulsion or anger—in this difficult area where "faith and human knowledge, faith and modem science, faith and the fight for justice" meet.

Second, and critically, the challenges of the future will be global challenges- the threat to our environment; global economic growth; the issues surrounding the migration of people in search of a better economic future; hunger, poverty, health, and disease— all of these are global issues that require solutions that transcend boundaries of nation, culture, and language. This may have always been true in fact, but now we live in a time when these boundaries are more porous than ever. I say to you that as people who would claim to be civil—and therefore to be responsible for our role in the upkeep of civilization—that we need to expand our understanding of what it means to be a citizen so that it has a global embrace. As you go on to study and to learn and to seek a career, I think you will be challenged to conceive of your place in the world as a global citizen, not just a citizen of the United States. This means we need to find ways to share our knowledge and resources with those areas of the world that need what we have to give.

Just as you would not let the person in the house next door starve to death, it is time for all of us who would hope to be considered civil, to embrace those suffering elsewhere in the world as our neighbors, and to accept that we have a responsibility, as global citizens for their welfare, and education.

Finally, what may be the greatest challenge to civility in the future is what Fr. Nicolás called "the globalization of superficiality." As he said: "When one can access o much information so quickly and so painlessly; when one can express and publish to the world one's reactions so immediately and so unthinkingly in one's blogs or micro-blogs; ... when the newest viral video can be spread so quickly to people half a world away, shaping their perception and feelings, then the laborious, painstaking world of serious, critical thinking often gets short-circuited."

All of you who have seen the recent film *The Social Network* about the rise of Facebook will know exactly what I'm talking about. Isn't it ironic that we can make friends with total strangers, learn everything about them, carry on intimate conversations, and then "de-friend" them with a click of a button?

When relationships are shaped in this way, without the "hard work of encounter, or if need be, confrontation and then reconciliation—then relationships can also become superficial."

I alluded in my introduction to the death of Tyler Clementi, the 18-year-old Rutgers student who committed suicide after his roommate posted pictures of him on the Internet. I'm sure you can all think of hundreds of other examples, perhaps in your own life, when the social media that binds you and connects you to others has also caused you pain and embarrassment, and made you feel unwanted and unimportant. The new social networks and technologies have not necessarily led to deeper relationships, or a greater appreciation of the dignity of the human person. Instead, they appear to have contributed to an ongoing objectification of human person. As Fr. Nicolás pointed out in his remarks to us in Mexico, the inner world of our students are being shaped by these technologies that emphasize immediate communication, but not necessarily deep communication, or true relationship. When that happens, people lose their ability to engage with reality as it is, or with other people in the fullness of who they are, and we find ourselves returning to an every-man-for-himself kind of culture, and to the shackles of barbarism.

I would suggest that "civility" in the 21st century

is going to require the hard work of finding, maintaining, and deepening real relationships with one another. This is why I believe that the model universities of the future will be places where there is as much emphasis placed on building community as there is on what goes on in the classroom. Certainly at Fairfield, we put our students together in living and learning communities with programs to ensure that they really get to know one another, that they have real relationships, that they understand that they have the potential to hurt other people by their actions, and to inspire them too.

We also create opportunities for our students to go out into the world as mentors and teachers, both in our surrounding communities and in service learning trips to the Philippines or Nicaragua, where they encounter their neighbors who need what they have to give. It's an amazing moment when a young man or women realizes that they can truly transform the life of a child by teaching them to read, or by encouraging them to write a poem. These real encounters are an important part of a liberal arts education now more than ever, because they cut across the "superficiality" of our culture and inspire true creativity in our students—the capacity to care, and hence to take responsibility for themselves as creative citizens in the world.

In closing: "Civility" as we understand it, is our inheritance—certainly the most priceless inheritance that we share as members of this society. For most of us, it is an inheritance that we pick up without any conscious effort, and so it is easy to fall under the impression that civility is fundamentally unassailable—carved in stone—and that it has always been at the heart of the way we have conducted ourselves. But this is not true. Civility as we understand it arose at a unique moment in our history, and has endured thanks to the men and women who have insisted over the centuries on a more civilized, compassionate, and just way of life than the barbarism that is the alternative. And there is no guarantee that this inheritance will continue unless men and women of vision insist that it do so.

At one time, perhaps, the barbarians were literally at the gate—and from time-to-time they are literally at the gate. But it is the casual barbarisms of our culture that—I would suggest—pose the biggest threat to our inheritance.

The temptation to abandon reason and tolerance in the face of aggressively hostile fundamentalisms, and to retreat into our own narrow definition of community; the refusal to extend civility to our neighbors who are suffering, impoverished, and in need of the knowledge and resources that we have in so much abundance; and the "globalization of superficiality" that is an undeniable dimension of the ways in which we have come to interact with one another, are among the biggest threats to our civil society in my view.

And as always, it seems to me, the surest way to

address these threats is through education. Education and civility are in a relationship of mutual dependence. Without education, our traditions will not endure, and if they do not endure, our appreciation of the value of a truly enriching education will likewise fall away. It is our schools and universities that are charged with the responsibility of forming young men and women so that they appreciate the inheritance that has been left for them, and so that they have the intellectual acumen, the passion for justice, and the depth of personhood, to extend the habit of civil behavior into these troubling frontiers that I have discussed today.

As educators, the responsibility falls to us to ensure that the students under are charge are offered the living and learning environments where they can discover the profundity of their own being, and so come to recognize the dignity of all God's creation and so their unique, personal responsibility to live and work in the service of their fellow men and women. If we apply ourselves to this responsibility earnest, then I believe we will not fail. I'm certain that the community of St. Charles Preparatory School shares my conviction in this matter, and as is so often the case with clergyman, I'm sure that I have found myself this afternoon preaching to the choir.

- November 12, 2010

In July 2004, the **REV. JEFFREY P. VON ARX, S.J.,** *became the eighth Jesuit to be named President of Fairfield University since the institution's founding in 1942.*

Father von Arx brings to Fairfield broad academic interests and an integrated view of learning. His zest for student life is born of having lived in undergraduate residence halls throughout his years at Georgetown and Fordham. His approach to the intellectual life reflects the best of what Jesuit education offers the world - the integration of knowledge and values as the foundation for unity of mind, body and spirit.

An historian by discipline, Father von Arx began his academic career at Georgetown University, where he taught in the History Department from 1982 to 1998, and was its chair from 1991 to 1997. He then moved into administration at Fordham University, serving as Dean of Fordham College at Rose Hill from 1998 until his selection as President by the Fairfield University Board of Trustees in 2004.

He graduated from Princeton University in 1969 and entered the Society of Jesus that summer. He subsequently earned an M.A. and M.Phil. in history at Yale University, and completed his Ph.D. there in 1980. A year later, Father von Arx received an M.Div. from the Weston School of Theology and was ordained a priest.

Father von Arx has served or is currently on the boards of trustees of Boston College, Canisius College, Loyola Marymount University and Xavier University, as well as Commission on Institutions of Higher Education (NEASC). He was appointed to the Fairfield Board in 2002 and as President continues to serve as a trustee.

10

William McGurn

on
Manliness

"A man is someone who will stand up for a principle he knows is right, as well as for people he sees are being picked on, even at great cost to himself. That does not mean he is without fear. Many a man's most courageous moment has come when he's been most afraid. A man is someone who does not let his fears conquer him."

When I accepted his invitation, I was pleased to learn that St. Charles is a school for young men. I will speak more about that later. Here I will just note that I am the father of three girls. Some of you students may be asking yourselves, "What does that mean?" Let me tell you what it means:

It means I have a keen interest in the formation of young men. It is an interest, moreover, that grows stronger and stronger as my daughters advance through their teenage years.

One of the men who has come from your ranks is a good friend of mine: Bob Dilenschneider. Bob is a straight shooter, a man I can always count on to tell me the truth. That may not mean much to you today. Someday, I promise you, it will. Right now I'd like to ask you join me in thanking Bob for his great love for this school – and for the high bar his example sets for all Carolians.

How fitting that this place of learning is named for St. Charles. The name Charles means "manly" or "strong." Manifestly that describes Charles Borromeo. He was a giant of the faith. In his own day, he was a bold and learned reformer who was even shot at by a disgruntled monk. Fortunately for history, the monk's shooting skills were apparently as deficient as his theology.

Your website says St. Charles offers you students "the opportunity to grow in Christian manhood." The handbook is quite specific about what it means by Christian manhood – "a personal relationship with God, accurate learning, and an ethic of disciplined work."

Not many institutions make that kind of claim these days. Would that more did. And that is precisely what I wish to talk with you about today: What it means to be a man in 21st century America.

When people say someone is manly, what do they mean? Most answers boil down to this: A man is someone who will stand up for a principle he knows is right, as well as for people he sees are being picked on, even at great cost to himself. That does not mean he is without fear. Many a man's most courageous moment has come when he's been most afraid. A man is someone who does not let his fears conquer him.

Manliness is not boastful, but it speaks a language understood by all. If you are a man, even those who are stronger than you will sense it. Even when they have defeated you, they will feel inferior in your presence. In like wise, if you are a fellow who cannot be counted on, everyone will soon know that too. Worst of all, you will know it yourself.

Today I'd like to share two examples of manhood. One was a soldier who was awarded the Medal of Honor. The other is a young father who has a little girl with Down syndrome. Each faced a moment of truth, when the easier thing would have been to look out for Number One. Each had the character to put love over self. Each in his own way shows what it means to be a man.

The soldier's name was Robert J. Miller. He was a sergeant in the Special Forces of the United States Army. In my time at the White House, I wrote several speeches commemorating men who were awarded the Medal of Honor. Sergeant Miller's medal was bestowed by President Obama, so I did not write those remarks. In the last year, however, I have learned much about this American fighting man from his mother.

The Medal of Honor is our nation's highest

award for valor. It is given for actions "above and beyond the call of duty." In other words, you cannot be awarded the Medal of Honor for something you were ordered to do, no matter how brave you might have been.

It tells you something about the Medal of Honor that seven of the ten men who have received it for their service in Iraq and Afghanistan were killed in the action that earned it. That's what we mean by "the last full measure of devotion." The United States bestows medals to acknowledge the extraordinary service and character of individuals who wear the uniform of our nation. Perhaps even more important, we give out medals to inspire the rest of us – to remind us what it means to take seriously words such as honor, and sacrifice, and courage.

In 2008, Sergeant Miller's unit was patrolling the Kunar province in northeastern Afghanistan. Their job was to root out Taliban forces that prey on innocent Afghan civilians. That winter night, Sergeant Miller and his fellow soldiers attacked an enemy compound. When they moved in closer to inspect the damage, they were ambushed by a larger Taliban force.

Instinctively, Sergeant Miller did two things. First, he attacked with everything he had. Second, he had the presence of mind to communicate the enemy's positions to the rest of his detachment so they could call in air support and better direct their fire. He did this even as he himself was returning fire.

As the battle unfolded, Sergeant Miller found himself farther up the mountain and much closer to the enemy positions than the 22 other men with him – 15 Afghans and 7 Americans. When his wounded commander called for the unit to pull back, Sgt. Miller saw that these men would not get out of that valley alive because they were pinned down by a much larger Taliban force. His answer was to charge the enemy again, exposing himself and drawing their fire. In so doing, he knew it would likely cost him his life – but he also knew it was the only way to save the lives of his brothers in arms.

Let me tell you something else about this Green Beret: He was only 24 years old when he died.

There was a day when our nation made movies about men like Sergeant Miller. This was one tough hombre, who liked his Scotch and liked his fast cars. At the core of his toughness, however, was an even tougher love: his love of freedom, his love of his nation, his love of others more than himself. He walked those unknown valleys in Afghanistan to keep people like us safe. And when his brother soldiers needed him most, he did what John: 15 tells us is the greatest of loves: to lay down his own life for his friends.

Sergeant Miller was also a Catholic boy, raised in what his mom tells me was a "home with a very clear sense of right and wrong." I'm not saying he was a saint. In fact, his mom tells me her son wasn't an easy child: He was willful, contrary, and sometimes reckless. Mrs. Miller puts it this way: "When we first started learning some of what happened when he died, even then we were wondering if his actions were deliberate and courageous – or more recklessness. As we found out more about the training that Special Forces go through and some of the actions that he had never told us about, it began to sink in that he knew exactly what he was doing up until his final moments."

In sum, Sergeant Miller was an individual whose manhood was forged in many fires: in the virtues nurtured by a loving home, in the disciplines instilled by the United States Special Forces, in the love of neighbor – the same chapter where Thomas Aquinas locates his treatment of warfare – rooted in his faith. When America was attacked on September 11, 2001, Robert Miller was a senior in high school. From the description Mrs. Miller gives me, he could have been any one of you St. Charles students here today.

Now, when I hear of stories like Sergeant Miller's, my admiration leaves me feeling frustrated. The reason is simple: There is no way I can ever even the score. I can't bring Sergeant Miller back to his family. I cannot even tell him "thank you." What I can do is this: to resolve to live a life worthy of this good man's sacrifice.

That is our challenge. And were he standing where I am today, Sergeant Miller would be the first to tell you that you don't have to wear a uniform to prove your manhood. There are other ways to be a man.

Matthew Hennessey is my other example. Though born Catholic, he grew up largely outside his church, and really didn't accept many of its teachings. In his twenties, he married a charming young woman named Ursula. They had a beautiful little girl named Clara. All signs pointed to a cozy future together.

Then the unexpected intervened. Ursula became pregnant again. A blood test four months into that pregnancy showed a 1 in 66 chance the baby had Down syndrome. Later an amnio test confirmed their worst fears.

Today Matthew says that when people meet his little girl, the first question many ask is this: Did they know before she was born? The implication, of course, is that only people who did not know would go on to have the baby. The implication is not far off: in America today, only one of ten children diagnosed with Down's makes it out of the womb.

In the last few decades, medical advances have raised the life expectancy of children with Down's from 25 to 55. We have conquered many of the medical complications associated with Down syndrome, including birth defects of the heart. And our society has created more opportunities for those with Down to live happy and fulfilling lives. Yet we are deliberately choosing to let fewer of them live.

Here's how Matthew answers the question whether he and his wife knew their child would be born with Down's: "We did know. And I can tell you that we didn't consider it a gift. At the time, we considered it a painful and confusing curse. We struggled for days and weeks to understand why God had selected us to carry this awful burden. We prayed for an easier path. We begged for it not to be true."

But it was true.

The news made agonizing what ought to have been a joyful period in their lives. At different times, Matthew and Ursula would become depressed, thinking of the things their as-yet unborn child would never be able to do. Somewhere in that fog, lying in bed one evening, Ursula turned to Matthew and blurted out: "You know we have to have it, you know?"

Without hesitation, Matthew replied, "Of course, I know. That's what I want too."

Men of St. Charles, let me emphasize that: *Without hesitation.*

That was Matthew's test. What came back from Ursula's question was more than an answer about this pregnancy. What came back was a liberating assurance: On the journey through life, she would not be alone. Standing beside her would be a man.

Earlier I mentioned how terrible it is for a fellow to look into the mirror and not like what he sees. The flip side is the peace that comes from doing the right thing. Of course, if you praised Matthew Hennessey for what he *"sacrificed"* to have his daughter, he'd tell you you're nuts. He'd tell you he has a beautiful little girl named Magdalena, named for the first woman to see the risen Christ. He would tell you that in the purity of each Magdalena smile, he catches a glimmer of the joy her namesake encountered outside that empty tomb.

I know a dozen other men who also have sons or daughters with Down Syndrome. They would tell you what Matthew would tell you: that they are not simply better men for these children, they are *happier* men.

Now, you here are young and single, so you may not fully appreciate what that means. *I*, by contrast, am *not* young and single. As the father of three girls, at the top of all my prayers is this one: That when a daughter of mine brings home the fellow she has given her heart to, he will be a man like Matthew. A man who will not run when life throws a curve.

I say this because the most striking characteristic of our society today is guys who run: guys who run from responsibility and remain children their whole lives, guys who run from marriage or fatherhood when they get tired of it, guys who get a girl pregnant and run her to the cold front door of an abortion clinic.

Yes, the ladies have their issues. But I'm not talking to ladies today. I'm talking to Carolians. You are here because the people who love you most have put you in a place where you might grow into Christian manhood.

My young friends, most of you will never patrol a dark valley in Afghanistan – or face the kind of news the Hennesseys did. Yet each of you will be tested.

The test will come in the everyday things of ordinary life: whether you are faithful to your wife, whether you are a father who puts his children before himself, whether you are honest and true with those you deal with. Most of all, it will come in those moments when you have a choice: to sit quietly on the sidelines – or to stand up for what's right and true, especially when standing up for what is right and true means mockery and derision and exclusion.

The good news is that you have a great advantage others do not. You have the witness of St. Charles – and the example of loving men and women who live its principles. At every turn on these beautiful grounds, you see that witness.

You see that witness in the stained-glass window of St. Francis that overlooks this commons and memorializes Kathleen Cavello, a woman who gave this institution her husband, her sons, and herself – because she knew how much our world needs strong, educated Christian men. You see that witness in your wonderful teachers, who so selflessly take their delight in your advancement. You see that witness in every issue of *The Cardinal*, with those splendid photos of men standing next to wives they have been married to for 40, 50, and 60 years. God willing, generations of St. Charles men yet unborn will see that same witness in the chapters you will write with your own lives.

Let me end with something our Pope once wrote about Charles Borromeo. He said: "Charles could convince others because he was a man of conviction. He was able to exist with his certitudes amid the contradictions of his time because he himself lived them. And he could live them because he was a Christian in the deepest sense of the word, in other words, he was totally centered on Christ."

My young Carolians, that is my hope for you. Bring your strength and conviction into a world that is hungry for them. Never be afraid to speak the name Jesus Christ. And in all you do, let your example lead your fellow citizens to say of these teachers and these halls: They took in boys, and they gave us back men.

- November 15, 2011

WILLIAM MCGURN *is editorial page editor of The New York Post.*

Previously he was a Vice President for News Corporation, where he wrote speeches for the CEO and the weekly "Main Street" column for The Wall Street Journal. From 2005 to 2008, he served as chief speechwriter for President Bush in the West Wing of the White House.

Prior to the White House, most of Mr. McGurn's career was in journalism. He was the chief editorial writer for the Wall Street Journal and spent more than 10 years overseas – in Europe and in Asia – for Dow Jones. He has also written for a wide variety of publications, from Esquire, the Washington Post and the New York Post to the Spectator of London and the National Catholic Register.

Bill is author of "Perfidious Albion: The Abandonment of Hong Kong 1997," as well as a monograph on terrorism. He is a member of the Council on Foreign Relations. He holds a bachelor's degree in philosophy from the University of Notre Dame, and a master's degree in communications from Boston University. And he has served on a variety of voluntary organizations, including the Presidential Commission on White House Fellows. Finally, he serves on the boards of Notre Dame's Center for Ethics and Culture, the social networking website Ricochet.com, and Ave Maria University in Florida.

Bill is married to the former Julie Hoffman, and they have three daughters: Grace, Maisie and Lucy. They now live in Madison, NJ.

AFTERWORD

My deepest gratitude to Bob Dilenschneider for this book and his support for the Borromean Lecture Series at St. Charles Preparatory School. His dedication to his high school alma mater is greatly appreciated and an inspiration to the students and faculty who attend the lectures each year. I hope the reader also has found the book equally interesting and inspiring.

I have spent my last forty-two years in education. In that time I have taught Latin, Greek, English and religion in this Roman Catholic high school. As an administrator and a teacher I had the opportunity to interact with thousands of young men both in and out of a classroom setting and I have taken my vocation as an educator and mentor most seriously.

The mission statement of St. Charles states that the administration and faculty are committed to modeling and making clear the importance of a personal relationship with God, accurate learning, and an ethic of disciplined work. I strongly believe that these three elements are critical components for molding competent young men into responsible adults.

The question is how to develop and nourish a passion for truth, beauty and goodness while the world around us tries its best to crowd out these ideals with alternatives that give us false choices. The most damaging choice I see today is the one which creates a "me first" mentality. It teaches that the primary importance of one's self-interest is to be regarded as the only path to a healthy, purposeful and meaningful life. As a result of the prevalence of this kind of thinking, we watch on our televisions and read in our papers daily the tragedy of war, greed, lack of compassion, and worst of all, incredible human ignorance; all driven by a selfishness that has little regard about how it may affect others.

As Bob pointed out in his introduction, the faculty of St. Charles served him well not only as teachers of the formal disciplines of his day but also as mentors and examples of how one should live his life. Their emphasis on students making a commitment to hard work, self-discipline, and personal responsibility has had a profound effect on him and countless others.

With the goal to produce mature young men who are effective decision-makers and who model Christian values in their relationships with others, the Borromean Lecture Series has proved to be a vital part of the educational program at St. Charles. When students are exposed to the movers and shakers of our government, church and major business institutions in such a personal way the result is often, as Bob says, "a lasting impact on my adolescent mind, the teachers who said something that resonated with me, the teachers who shared an eternal truth that I carried with me into adulthood which changed me forever."

My sincere hope, since our mission is so critical,

is that the Borromean Lecture Series continues for many more years to educate and inspire the future leaders of our community.

- Dominic J. Cavello
  Principal Emeritus, St. Charles Preparatory School

About the Editor, Robert L. Dilenschneider

Robert L. Dilenschneider is Founder and Principal of The Dilenschneider Group.

Prior to forming his own firm, Mr. Dilenschneider served as president and chief executive officer of Hill and Knowlton, Inc. from 1986 to 1991, tripling that Firm's revenues to nearly $200 million and delivering more than $30 million in profit. Mr. Dilenschneider was with that organization for nearly 25 years.

Mr. Dilenschneider started in public relations in 1967 in New York, shortly after receiving an M.A. in journalism from Ohio State University, and a B.A. from the University of Notre Dame.

Experienced in a number of communications disciplines, Mr. Dilenschneider is frequently called upon by the media to provide commentary and strategic public relations insights on major news stories. He has counseled major corporations, professional groups, trade associations and educational institutions, and has assisted clients in dealings with regulatory agencies, labor unions, consumer groups and minorities, among others.

Mr. Dilenschneider is a member of the advisory board of the Center for Strategic and International Studies and sits on the Board of Governors of the New York Chapter of the National Academy of Television Arts and Sciences and the North American Advisory Board of The Michael Smurfit School of

Business at University College, Dublin. Mr. Dilenschneider is a member of The Bretton Woods Committee, a trustee of the Institute of International Education, a member of the American Lung Association's
President's Council, and a former member of the
Board of Governors of the American Red Cross. He
is a member of the Soundwaters Honorary Board,
and serves as a judge for The Olin Award, a program
of the Olin School of Business at Washington University in St. Louis. He has served on numerous
corporate boards.

Mr. Dilenschneider is a member of the Council
on Foreign Relations, the U.S.-Japan Business Council, the Economic Clubs of New York and Chicago,
and the Florida Council of 100. He also is a member
of the Public Relations Society of America, the International Public Relations Association and a member
of the Advisory Board of the Florence Biennale of
Cultural Heritage and Landscape. He is a Fellow to
the International Association of Business Communi-
cators. In recognition of his contribution in promoting New York City, Mr. Dilenschneider received the
City's Big Apple award. In 2001, he received an honorary Doctorate of Public Service degree from Musk-
ingum College, and in 2012 he received an honorary
Doctorate of Humane Letters from the University of
New Haven. Mr. Dilenschneider has been called the
"Dean of American Public Relations Executives" and
is widely published, having authored twelve books,
including the best selling *A Briefing for Leaders, On*

Power, The Critical 14 Years of Your Professional Life, Moses: C.E.O, The Critical 2nd Phase of your Professional Life, 50 Plus!—Critical Career Decisions for the Rest of Your Life, A Time for Heroes, and most recently, *Power and Influence: The Rules Have Changed.* He has lectured before scores of professional organizations and colleges, including the University of Notre Dame, Ohio State University, New York University and The Harvard Business School.

He attended St. Charles Preparatory School and graduated in 1961.

Made in the USA
Charleston, SC
05 November 2013